REACHING HIGHER

BILLY OLSON

REACHING HIGHER

with
CARLTON
STOWERS

WORD BOOKS
PUBLISHER
WACO, TEXAS

A DIVISION OF
WORD, INCORPORATED

BILLY OLSON: REACHING HIGHER
Copyright © 1984 by
Word Incorporated, Waco, Texas.

Scripture quotations in this
book are from the King James Version of the Bible.

Library of Congress Cataloging in Publication Data:

Olson, Billy, 1958–
  Reaching higher.

    1. Olson, Billy, 1958–   . 2. Track and field
athletes — United States — Biography. 3. Vaulting.
4. Christian biography—United States. I. Stowers,
Carlton. II. Title.
GV697.047A37   1984   796.4'32'0924   [B]   84-7560
ISBN 0–8499–0387–4

Printed in the United States of America

To my parents and family, whom I love very much, and to the special people of Abilene, who have always been supportive.

B. O.

To my sister, Laurie, who always was an Abilene girl.

C. S.

Contents

Foreword

FOR OVER A DECADE Bob Richards ruled as the dominant figure in the sport of pole vaulting, claiming 11 consecutive national indoor championships and 10 outdoors. Three times he was a member of the United States Olympic team, earning a bronze medal in 1948 at the London Games before claiming back-to-back Olympic championships in 1952 and 1956. In winning his gold medals—the only time anyone has ever won the event twice in the Olympics—he established new Games records. In 1952, in Helsinki, he raised the standard to 14 feet, 11½ inches. Four years later, in Melbourne, he added another quarter inch to his own record.

Long before the fiberglass pole came into play and began hurling vaulters to celestial heights, Richards, a graduate of the University of Illinois, cleared 15 feet no fewer than 126 times. Additionally, he was an athlete of such versatility that he claimed three national decathlon championships. In all, he can look back on 25 national titles in track-and-field competition.

In 1951, he received the Sullivan Award, which goes annually to the most outstanding amateur athlete in the United States.

And he's not yet through. Just last summer Richards felt the competitive urges again surfacing and began training to participate in the fast-growing age-group Masters Track and Field program. In Puerto Rico, at age 57, he won his specialty at the World Championships. That title, earned 27 years after his second Olympic crown, came just weeks after he was honored as one of the 20 charter members of the United States Olympic Hall of Fame.

9

Some years ago, I had the privilege of speaking at a huge Christian Crusade in Abilene, Texas, along with radio commentator Paul Harvey and humorist Jerry Clower. I was giving my usual speech which pertained to great Olympic athletes and how they became winners, stressing the motivational aspect of sports.

In the audience that night was a young man 16 years of age who had what I've always called the "look of an eagle." He had set his sights on becoming a world-record holder in the pole vault.

I have seen many young men and women who have decided to dedicate themselves to become champions at an early age. Among them are Mark Spitz, the magnificent swimmer who won a record seven gold medals at the Olympic Games in Munich; figure skater Peggy Fleming, who earned the United States's only gold medal at the '68 Winter Games in Grenoble; others like Billie Jean Moffit and Rafer Johnson. The list is long and impressive.

That night in Abilene, I met Billy Olson for the first time and decided then and there that he was going to be not only a world-record holder, but an Olympic champion as well. As a matter of fact, during my speech I had Billy stand and I prognosticated that very night that he would become one of our great champions and would win the pole vault in the Olympics one day. Later, on a couple of occasions when I served as honorary referee at track-and-field meets being held at Abilene Christian University, I said the same thing over the public address system.

Now the 1984 Olympic Games are drawing near and I think Billy, along with sprinter/long jumper Carl Lewis and hurdler Edwin Moses, is our best prospect for a gold medal at Los Angeles.

If he does make my prophecy come true, it could happen to no nicer or more deserving person. In addition to his remarkable athletic achievements, Billy Olson has had a tremendous influence for good among young people. I have noticed in many interviews how articulate he is and how unselfishly he always refers to his coach and other teammates and to their greatness rather than his own.

Beyond being an athlete, he is an outstanding individual. In fact, I can only hope my own children will grow into the kind of person Billy Olson is.

In my estimation, he perfectly fulfills the scripture found in

Isaiah: "They that wait upon the Lord shall renew their strength; they shall mount up with wings as eagles; they shall run, and not be weary; and they shall walk, and not faint" (Isa. 40:31).

Whatever height Billy Olson might one day reach in pole vaulting will be secondary to the height he achieves as a human being in the greatest game of all—the game of living.

—BOB RICHARDS

Preface

THE SCENE WAS a crowded Dallas Cowboys dressing room on an afternoon before the team was to go through yet another practice as it prepared for the National Football League play-offs. In virtually every corner, the subject was the same: reporters were talking with players and coaches about the upcoming game, gathering material for the next day's editions.

Having spent a number of my professional years in the presence of athletes, football players in particular, I must admit there is little new information to be learned from such conversations. The news story angles get harder and harder to come by. There are times, in fact, when the chore becomes downright tedious—for the interviewer and for those being interviewed.

In something more akin to desperation than inventiveness, reporters find themselves seeking out the offbeat topics at every opportunity. Thus it was that I was talking with Butch Johnson, a veteran wide receiver for the Cowboys, about a subject we had not previously explored.

My mission on this particular visit to the Cowboys' practice facility was to gather information on the varied athletic backgrounds of team members. I had found, for instance, that center Tom Rafferty had been a prep All-America lacrosse player, that quarterback Danny White had played the infield well enough at Arizona State to be offered a big-league contract, and that Ed (Too Tall) Jones had been a far better basketball player than defensive end as a schoolboy and collegian back in Tennessee.

Then Butch surprised me with his recollections of his California

13

days as a high-school pole-vault champion. It had, in fact, been pole vaulting, not pass catching, which had earned him a college scholarship. (At the time he was unaware that I was working on the book now in your hands, thus the testimonial to follow was given without benefit of unfair coaxing.)

"People have no idea," he was saying, "just how much athletic ability pole vaulting requires. You've got to have tremendous speed, strength, and coordination—and enough nerve to jump out of a two-story building. Take Billy Olson, for instance. There probably isn't a greater athlete in the world than that guy. The things he's done in the past few years—getting the world indoor record up to 19 feet, consistently vaulting at heights most of his competition doesn't even think about trying—amaze me. If I had to pick the athlete I admire above all others today, Olson is the one."

Butch Johnson and I have not always seen eye-to-eye on things, but in this instance we were in perfect agreement.

Working with Billy on his book has been, if you'll pardon the triteness, a tremendously rewarding experience—in more ways than one. I have been able to relive a great many moments of superior athletic accomplishment with him as we prepared the manuscript, and I have also learned a great deal about the motivation of a person who dedicates himself to excellence in a sport which all too rarely enjoys the national spotlight. Most importantly, I have become acquainted with a young man who has overcome difficulties to become something more than a highly regarded world-class athlete. In a world tragically short of role models, I offer Billy Olson, athlete and person, as one worthy of emulation.

The preparation of this manuscript has also been something of a nostalgic journey for me.

When Word Editorial Director Ernie Owen put Billy Olson and me together on this project, he probably didn't realize he was proposing an undertaking with which I felt more comfortable than almost any I'd ever launched. Having grown up in Abilene, Texas, attended Abilene High School, and been a member of the track team which won a state championship (about a lifetime before Billy Olson began setting records there), I had firsthand knowledge of the lay of the land Billy calls home.

Like Billy, I had had good times growing up in West Texas. And

*as he reflected on his teenage years, there were times when I felt
swept even further back to a more carefree day—a day when performing well in the San Angelo Relays and talking my dad out of
the keys to the car were among life's greatest concerns.*

*And, like Billy, I have climbed the fence which surrounded the
track at Abilene Christian College (now Abilene Christian University), there to run on the hallowed turf of one of my boyhood heroes.*

*It was in 1956, at the Olympic Games in Melbourne, that Abilene
Christian's Bobby Morrow won three gold medals—in the 100
meters, 200 meters and as a member of the four-by-100-meter relay.
Never had my hometown had such a celebrity. And never have I
ached and prayed so to be like someone else.*

Which brings me to a confession long overdue.

*On a long-ago holiday weekend visit to the deserted ACU track, a
friend and I discovered the dressing room had been unlocked. We
welcomed ourselves in. There, in all its glory, we found the uniform
Bobby Morrow, the World's Fastest Human, had worn during his
triumphs in Melbourne.*

*My accomplice raced for the car to get his camera while I quickly
changed into the only United States Olympic team uniform I would
ever wear. Somewhere, well hidden, I still have that snapshot of a
skinny 16-year-old kid standing there, chest expanded, living out a
fantasy which never had a chance to become a reality.*

There! I feel better that the story is out. My apologies, Bobby.

*Billy Olson, I'm convinced, will never have to resort to such tac-
tics. The Olympic uniform he will wear will be his own. It is something I look foward to almost as much as he does.*

—CARLTON STOWERS

*Maturity is your ability to see
into tomorrow the results of your
actions today, and to choose those
actions accordingly. . . .*

—Sign in Abilene Christian
University track dressing room

1

A Cold Night in Toronto

DRIVING SLEET, looking like so many crystal BBs, beat down and bounced crazily off the wings of the commercial airliner as it finally touched down in Toronto. A stewardess apologized that the plane was two hours late arriving and warned of the temperature outside. It was, the all-too-cheery voice said, 15 degrees Fahrenheit, with a chill factor considerably lower.

Billy Olson, weary from a journey that had begun early in the morning, had not waited for the intercom weather report. Even as the plane taxied toward the terminal he had taken a wool knit cap from his carry-on bag and pulled it hard down over his ears.

He knew what to expect of February in Canada.

Stepping into the midnight air, I felt the knifing Canadian wind and cold cut through me as if the coat I was wearing were made of tissue paper. Maybe the stewardess had meant to say *minus* 15. Even inside the terminal, which was almost totally deserted, the cold air surrounded me. I couldn't help but think of how warm and comfortable my apartment back in Abilene, Texas, would be.

But I was really glad to be there. For several weeks I had been looking forward to competing in the *Toronto Star*-Maple Leaf Indoor Games, privately fantasizing about the returning hero's welcome I was sure to receive upon my arrival. It had been there, a year earlier, that I had improved the world record in the pole vault to 18 feet, 8¾ inches. The meet directors, worried about attendance problems and the very future of the meet (one of the oldest and most respected on the indoor track-and-field circuit), had insisted my world record had been the shot in the arm they needed.

And in one of those important bursts of optimism to which athletes are subject, I had told them I would be back next year to try and break the record again.

This time, I had already been advised, a crowd of 12,000 or more would be on hand to watch me try to live up to my promise. The fact that I had improved on my own world record twice in the early weeks of the indoor season—first in Ottawa, then at the Sunkist Invitational in Los Angeles, where I had vaulted 18 feet, 10¾ inches—had not been overlooked by the Toronto media or the meet promoters.

The word was out that Billy Olson was coming to town to set another world record. I felt a little like an Old-West fast gun riding into town to take on all challengers. Frankly, I was feeling pretty good about myself.

Until I realized there was no one at the near-deserted airport to meet me.

Not that I expected a brass band, mind you. But one of the arrangements meet directors generally make is to have someone meet you upon arrival to help you get to the hotel. Pole vaulters, you have to understand, don't travel light. In addition to my luggage, I had four 16½-foot vaulting poles with me. They aren't something you can simply tuck under your arm and stroll through the terminal with.

Suffice it to say my ego was snapped quickly back into place. The fast gun was beginning to feel a lot like little boy lost.

To get to Toronto I had driven 200 miles from Abilene to Dallas, the poles tied onto the top of my car. Then, after the always-hectic chore of getting the poles to the freight area at Dallas-Fort Worth International Airport and repeatedly insisting to the baggage handlers how important it was that they didn't wind up in Chicago or Pittsburgh, I had made my customary dash for the ticket counter. And learned that the weather had forced a two-hour delay in takeoff. Making some kind of sarcastic remark about the glamor of travel, I had gone in search of the terminal newsstand. There's a lot of hurrying-up-and-waiting in the pole-vault business.

Obviously, whoever was to have met me in Toronto had given up and gone home, imagining I was hopelessly snowbound some-where and never going to make it. As I waited for my poles to be delivered to me, I envisioned my welcome committee at home, tucked into a warm bed.

Then I went in search of an understanding cab driver.

It didn't take long to realize that the one I found was several light years removed from being the greatest pole-vault fan in the world. The problem of attaching the tools of my trade to his cab wasn't one he was outwardly enthusiastic about dealing with. But I promised big bucks and we were on our way.

It was one o'clock in the morning when I finally got to bed, aching from head to toe, feeling like a man who badly needed ten years' sleep. But the hard part was over. I had arrived. Now all I had to do was go out the next evening and live up to the expecta-tions of 12,000 fans who had been assured I was going to do some-thing spectacular.

I dreamed, not of world records, but of arriving at the meet only to realize I had forgotten to bring a uniform or track shoes with me. The last thing I remember dreaming was that I told the meet officials I would have to vault in my jeans and street shoes and that they could forget about any world record.

The Maple Leaf Garden, to be frank, looks like something urban renewal overlooked. Earl Bell, a pole-vaulting friend of mine, once said that it was probably ten years out of date when World War II broke out. The boards of the track are badly chewed up and crack-ing, and there is little color or warmth to the place. But, for reasons I can't really explain, it is a favored place among vaulters. The runway is ideal, the lights are focused on the landing pit, and everything looks perfect when you're standing at the top of the course, preparing for a vault.

Twice previously I had cleared personal record heights in the Garden. Frankly, I was feeling good about my chances of doing just what the meet promoters had been saying I might do. In fact, when I did an interview with CBS-TV the morning before the meet, I had to caution myself repeatedly not to sound too confident.

Instead, I talked of the record-setting jumps I had managed in the previous weeks, said I was a little surprised to be vaulting so well so early in the season, and said, yes, I did feel a 19-foot vault was lurking somewhere in the near future.

"Like maybe tonight?" the interviewer asked. "We'll just have to wait and see." I did everything but flash a knowing wink into the camera. The ham in me always seems to get the last word.

The day of a competition is always endless. I'm no sightseer and have no interest in going out to movies or museums, so I spend the day being as inactive as I possibly can: staying in the hotel, napping, reading, playing cards, and talking with friends—about anything but the meet.

I don't allow myself early in the day to get too involved thinking about what I hope to do, for the simple reason that I get nervous. Most athletes are that way. Find a group of world-class track-and-field athletes the afternoon before they are to compete, and you might immediately assume they don't care whether they do well or not. There's always a lot of laughing and horsing around. Everybody's loose, their minds a million miles removed from competing.

Actually, it is just part of the preparation process we all go through.

One thing unique to pole vaulting is the fact that vaulters hang around together constantly. It's like being part of a traveling fraternity. There's none of the "I'm going to avoid that guy because he's the enemy" stuff in the sport. Rather, we help each other, making suggestions about technique, loaning each other poles, sharing training philosophy, and offering encouragement. The reason for this somewhat unusual athletic camaraderie is that other vaulters are the only people in the world who understand what we do!

So, up until about ten minutes before we were to leave for the arena, I sat in the hotel room talking with Earl Bell (the vaulter I would likely have the greatest difficulty beating).

Finally, he stood up, stretched, and said, "Okay, let's start growling at each other a little. It's showtime." We laughed, gathered our gear, and headed in the direction of the Maple Leaf Garden. Mercifully, the waiting was almost over.

In the newspaper rack outside the hotel entrance, a headline caught my eye: "Olson Eyes World Record in Garden Tonight."

It was time, I knew, to begin getting nervous.

The most common—and most justified—criticism of the event in which I've chosen to compete is that it often takes forever and a day to complete. At the 1964 Olympic Games in Tokyo, for instance, the pole-vault finals got underway at one in the afternoon with a bright, warm sun shining. Then they proceeded to move with exasperating slowness as officials raised the bar only two inches at a time during the eliminations. It was ten that night when Texan Fred Hansen cleared 16 feet, 8¾ inches on his third and final try to win the gold medal and set a new Olympic record.

Nine hours! It had only taken Ethiopia's Abebe Bikila two hours and 12 minutes to earn his gold medal in the marathon.

While things have improved some in recent years, the basic format of pole vaulting has remained the same. Each entrant has three opportunities to clear each height. If he fails in three tries, he's out. If you have a large field with a number of vaulters starting at the lower heights and then having difficulty making them, the match can become pretty tedious for those who are capable of clearing greater heights. What you do, then, is just pass until the bar reaches a height at which you feel comfortable entering the competition. It's more a matter of conserving energy than anything. In my case, for instance, there is no reason for me to vault at 17 feet when I've been clearing 18 or better for several years.

Because of that, it is often 45 minutes to an hour after the pole-vault competition has begun before I actually make my first jump. And with that in mind, I try to gauge my warmups accordingly.

In Toronto, I had decided I would make my first attempt when the bar reached 18 feet, ½ inch. But, for one of the rare times in my competitive life, the event moved along swiftly. When the bar reached the height at which I had decided to enter, I wasn't properly warmed up. I had spent too much time playing the role of fan, watching the three-ring circus of events going on around me.

I told the officials that I would pass until the bar was raised again—to 18 feet, 4½ inches. Tim Bright, a former teammate of mine at Abilene Christian University who had cleared 17 feet, 6½ inches (third place) before bowing out, looked at me as if I were crazy.

I just shrugged and got busy warming up.

When I did enter the competition, then, only Earl Bell and I were still in contention. On my second attempt at 18 feet, 4½ inches, I cleared it. Bell also succeeded at the height, and the bar was raised to 18-8.

Then Tom Jennings, coach of the Pacific Coast Club for which I now compete, called me over and asked how I felt about going for the record. I told him I thought it was possible, but not if I had to make a lot of vaults to get there.

He suggested I should go ahead and jump at 18-8. It would, he suggested, be a good progression. I thought about it for a minute and then told him I would just be wasting my time. If I was going for the record, there was no use fooling around with a height I felt sure I could make. Getting over 18-4 had given me a feel for what I could do. I would wait it out.

Coach Jennings gave no indication whether he thought I was doing the right thing. And when the public-address announcer informed the crowd that I was passing at 18-8, you could hear the groans. I don't think there was a person in the arena who wasn't convinced I was stark, raving loony.

Earl Bell failed in his three attempts at 18-8, and I was declared the winner of the competition by virtue of fewer misses at earlier heights. Then the official in charge of the pole vault came over to me and asked to what height I would like to have the bar raised.

The number was one I had had in mind long before beginning my drive to Dallas the day before. In fact, it was one I had been thinking about for a couple of years. The height I had in mind would establish me as the best pole vaulter in the world.

I told them to put the bar at 19 feet, ¼ inch. No one needed to remind me that in the history of the sport 19 feet had never been attained indoors.

Earl Bell recalls, "It didn't surprise me at all that Billy was going to take a shot at 19 feet in Toronto. It's the ideal place to do it. There's something almost mystical about the place; the runway is great, the atmosphere is right, and they've always placed a great deal of attention on the pole vault at that meet.

"I had seen him make a try at 19 in the Los Angeles Sports Arena a couple of weeks earlier and, frankly, he wasn't too aggressive

about it. He made one unsuccessful attempt and called it a night.
Maybe he knew the time just wasn't right. Or maybe he didn't want
to fail at it three times and begin to doubt that he could, in fact, make
it.

"He never mentioned it the day of the meet while we were sitting
around, shooting the bull, but I knew what he was thinking. I didn't
say anything either, but I kept thinking to myself, 'Billy, you're
never going to find a better setup than they have right here, so you
had better make up your mind to go for it.'"

When I stepped onto the runway to make my first jump at the
record, you could have heard a pin drop. Chapel services back at
Abilene Christian had never been so hushed. Even Earl and Tim,
who had pulled on their warmups and had been offering me all
kinds of advice, stood silently by, waiting for my vault. I don't
remember ever preparing for a jump in such silence. It was almost
as if I were suddenly sealed in a vacuum, isolated in a little world of
my own—just me, the 90 feet of runway, and a bar 19 feet above the
floor.

My first attempt looked more like a public suicide attempt.

My speed down the runway had been good. I had planted the pole
solidly in the box and had ridden the bend in the pole just the way I
had hoped to. But as I made my turn over the bar I began to fade to
one side. And suddenly the thing which pole vaulters try to block
from their minds—fear—took over. A world record was no longer
my concern. I was falling sideways and not at all sure where I was
going to land.

Fortunately, my body caught the edge of the foam rubber pit,
which cushioned my fall. I hit, then rolled off onto the concrete
floor of the arena. Another foot to the side, and I'm convinced I
would have broken both legs.

Officials and athletes who had been standing nearby rushed up
to see if I was all right. Physically, I was fine. Mentally, I was a
wreck. For a moment I considered telling the officials that I didn't
want to make another try. Instead, I went over to where the high-
jump pit was still in place and stretched out, trying to calm myself.
For several minutes I lay there, shaking. Then I began to feel
calmer. It was just one of those fluke things that happens now and

then, I told myself. I lay there for almost 15 minutes, shutting the aborted attempt out of my mind. Then, finally, I began to mentally picture my second try.

Everything had been right the first time except my arch over the bar. Actually, I had cleared the bar but had knocked it off when I lost balance coming down.

I got up and began to stretch, to loosen any muscles which might have tightened while I was lying down. I waved to the crowd and smiled, indicating all was well and that I was going to have another go at it.

The second time around, the crowd reaction was different. Suddenly I had a full house of cheerleaders. They applauded, shouted encouragement. Bell approached me at the top of the runway, smiling. "This is the one," he said.

As I think back on it today, I remember the jump in slow motion—going down the runway, planting the pole, arching up and over. I nicked the bar ever so slightly as I pushed the pole away, but it stayed in place. Then I was falling, this time dead center into the mat.

I knew I had made it even before I hit the pit.

And as I lay there, offering up a prayer of thanks, a deafening roar traveled through the Garden. People were standing, cheering, waving their arms. Everything seemed to go crazy for a few minutes. One of the officials rushed up to help me out of the pit and hugged me, then suggested I take a victory lap around the track.

I've never enjoyed a run more. The 19-foot barrier was behind me. At that moment I was certain it would no longer stand in my way. I would go higher.

But not on that night. I declined the offer to attempt another height. Suddenly, I felt drained. The flow of adrenalin had completely stopped. All I wanted to do was shower and get to bed, to savor the moment for a while—and then get ready to try it all over again the next night.

The *Dallas Times-Herald* indoor meet, scheduled less than 24 hours away, was something I had been looking forward to for quite some time. Some very special people were going to be in the stands, and I was determined to do well for them.

Turning down offers to celebrate, I went straight to bed. It was almost one o'clock, and for the next couple of hours I lay there, recreating the jump in my mind. I kept telling myself, *You've finally done it. The goal you set has been reached. Now it's time to reevaluate and set new goals. First of all, you should be jumping at 19 feet in every meet you enter. You made it once, you can do it again.*

Even though sleep came slowly and my seven-o'clock wake-up call came early, I had a good feeling about things as I headed back to Texas.

With his performance in Toronto on that night of 4 February 1983, Billy Olson had improved on the world indoor pole-vault record for a seventh time in a 12-month span of time. He had first claimed the mark, which had been co-owned by Konstantin Volkov of the Soviet Union and Thierry Vigneron of France, in February of 1982, clearing 18-8¾. By the end of the season he had elevated the record to 18-10.

Then in 1983 he had broken his own record first in Ottawa, then in Los Angeles, before his 19-¼ leap in the Maple Leaf Garden.

His triumph elevated him into an elite group of only three men who have ever cleared 19 feet in the event. In June of 1981 Thierry Vigneron of France had upped the outdoor world mark to 19-¼, and six days later Russia's Vladimir Polyakov had improved the mark to 19-¾.

On Wednesday nights for the past couple of years I had been helping conduct discussions with a group of eighth- and ninth-grade students in our church. There are 18 kids in the group, and we would get together and just talk about the problems of growing up, the importance of a Christian life, and all the different feelings they are wrestling with. There are times, quite honestly, when I'm not sure who is teaching whom. These kids are so much smarter than I was at their age. Still, having been something of a rebel and troublemaker at their age, I felt maybe I could be of some help to them.

For some time it had been planned for the entire group to make the trip to Dallas to watch me vault. Jeff and Tammie Utter, friends of mine who were also involved in the Wednesday night huddle sessions, would drive them up from Abilene.

It goes without saying that I wanted to perform well with "my" kids in the stands.

Having anticipated that I wouldn't get much rest the night before, I had devised a plan to get some much-needed sleep upon arriving in Dallas. Instead of going to the hotel where most of the athletes were being housed, I went directly to a friend's house. Away from reporters and everyone else who might want to talk about my new world record, I slept all afternoon. I woke at four and had something to eat, then just sat around watching television and reading the newspaper until time to report to Reunion Arena.

But, as so often is the case, the best laid plans often go awry when you're competing on the indoor track circuit. According to the schedule the pole vault was to get underway at seven in the evening. But when I arrived at the arena, Earl Bell and Dan Ripley met me with angered looks on their faces.

A number of athletes who had competed in the *Los Angeles Times* indoor meet the night before were having difficulty getting from L.A. to Dallas. To accommodate them, the entire schedule had been rearranged and the pole vault wouldn't begin for another hour and a half.

It is difficult to explain, but to me there is nothing more physically draining than sitting around waiting. Still, there was nothing else to do since I was already there. I did a little jogging to get the kinks out of my muscles, then sought out Jeff and Tammie and the group from Abilene and went to sit with them in the stands. With time on my hands, I decided to just enjoy the meet.

Soon I was cheering right along with the crowd of over 12,000. Carl Lewis, the remarkable sprinter and long jumper from Houston, had decided to run his first 60-yard dash in something like two years and proceeded to establish a new world record. And Mary Decker, the finest woman distance runner the United States has ever had, looked magnificent as she easily won the mile run.

From my vantage point in the stands, it was easy to see why people so enjoy indoor track meets. The close proximity to the action, the fact that several events are going on at the same time, and the pomp and color of the indoor meets makes for great the-

ater. Anyone who disputes the fact that athletes are in the enter-
tainment business need only to attend an indoor track meet to
have their minds changed in a hurry.

The field in the pole vault was much the same as it had been the
night before in Toronto—Earl Bell and Tim Bright were both
there. So was Dan Ripley, who had set the indoor record back in
1976, lost it for a couple of years to vaulters from Poland, then had
reclaimed it in 1979. And there was a delegation of Japanese
vaulters, led by Tomomi Takahashi.

I honestly can't remember ever being as fired up for a meet.
Intellectually, I knew I was tired and probably didn't have that
many good jumps in me. But I felt ready and eager, thinking that I
might even have a chance to get over 19 feet again. The fact that I
had so many friends in the stands was a big boost. And while I had
won the Dallas meet the year before with a vault of 18 feet, ½ inch,
I hadn't felt I performed well. I was eager to do better this time
around.

But not so anxious that I would enter the competition early.
Again I decided to bide my time and this time decided to wait until
the bar was raised to 18 feet, 4½ inches.

For a while, when I began to jump, I doubted my own judgment.
Despite the unbelievable response of the crowd, it took me three
jumps to clear my opening height. As I stood at the end of the
runway, preparing to make my third jump, the chilling thought
that I might miss, might not clear any height at all, ran through
my mind.

It wasn't the kind of jump the sportswriters are likely to write
any poems about, but I managed to get over on that third attempt.
The jump assured me of first place since Earl had settled for a best
of 18 feet, ½ inch.

The bar was raised to 18-8¾. Again it took me three jumps to
clear it. I was totally exhausted, going on a touch of madness and a
lot of determination. What I would have liked to do was sack up my
poles, put on my warmups, and call it a night.

But I knew that wasn't what the people had come to see. I asked
the officials to raise the bar to 19 feet, ¾ inches. Might as well have
another go at the record.

Ninety-five percent of the time, I know in the last three or four steps of my approach whether I'm going to clear the bar or not. It's just one of those instinctive feelings you have after years of vaulting. On that night I never really felt good about my chances of clearing 19-¾, despite the fact I came close twice. I just felt like I was running on an empty tank.

Still, it was good to win. And while I'm sure a lot of people went home disappointed in the fact I hadn't set a world record, the height I did clear was better than any other vaulter has ever done indoors.

All in all, it was a successful evening.

The greeting I received from the kids afterwards would have made you think I had vaulted 20 feet. Following the meet we all went across the street to the hotel and had a midnight dinner. They were all hugging me and telling me how proud they were of me. It was as great a feeling as setting the world record.

We sat there for a long time, eating, talking, laughing. All the pressures of the weekend had vanished, and it was a great feeling to relax with friends and not worry about another meet for a few days.

As we prepared to leave, Jeff Utter called me aside and shook my hand. "Billy," he said, "these kids really love you."

I laughed and said, jokingly, "Yeah, but they would probably have had my head if I'd failed tonight—and I almost did, you know."

"Billy," he said, "the fact you're the best pole vaulter in the world has little to do with how those kids in there feel about you. The guy they like is Billy Olson, person—someone who cares about them. That's what makes you special."

I had no clever answer for that. Just a very warm feeling.

The demands of the Toronto-to-Dallas weekend took their toll on Olson. Returning to Abilene, he stayed in bed for three days. Exhausted physically and mentally, he did not even work out. Concerned that he might be ill, he even visited the doctor. After an examination the doctor told him there was nothing wrong that rest wouldn't cure. "You're in excellent condition," he said, "but your body is just worn out. It's telling you it needs some rest."

Indeed, there was justification. With the 1983 indoor season only a month old, Olson had accomplished an amazing string of victories. In Ottawa he had cleared 18-10¼, at the Sunkist Invitational in Los Angeles he had gone 18-10¾, and at the Millrose Games in New York's Madison Square Garden he had won with a vault of 18 feet, 4½ inches.

Then had come the world record in Toronto and his victory in Dallas.

His college coach, Don Hood, suggested that maybe it was time to take a weekend off. Billy agreed.

But that was on Wednesday. Thursday he was feeling better. Friday night he was in San Francisco, where he delighted the crowd with a winning leap of 18-6¾.

"Billy is one of those special athletes who is never satisfied with what he's done," says Hood. "There is a drive inside him that you don't coach into an athlete. He's a competitor. I honestly think he wakes every day certain he's going to be better than he was the day before. And he wants to prove that to the world.

"To prove it, he has to compete, to constantly work to go higher. His dedication is incredible."

But it wasn't always so. Time was when Bill Olson, Sr. and his wife Barbara wondered if their son would ever move his life in a positive direction. . . .

2

Father and Son

THE HALLMARK FAMILY next door had ordered new carpet for their living room, giving absolutely no thought to the possibility that their decision might one day be looked back on as a significant moment in sports history. The carpet arrived wrapped around a 12-foot-long bamboo pole that looked a great deal like the one world pole-vault record holder Cornelius Warmerdam had used to scale remarkable heights in the '40s.

Billy Olson knew about Warmerdam, the man many considered the greatest pole vaulter in history. He had read about him and seen his picture in the World Book Encyclopedia. Between 1940 and 1944, Warmerdam, using a bamboo pole wrapped with tape, had cleared 15 feet no fewer than 43 times. No other vaulter in the world had been able seriously to challenge him. In fact, it had been seven years after his retirement before anyone else had managed to clear the height he routinely accomplished.

Eleven-year-old Billy wasted no time inviting young friend Mark Hallmark to come over and bring the pole with him. And soon the two youngsters were racing the length of the Olson backyard, balancing the pole clumsily as they went, and vaulting over a makeshift bar.

Barbara Olson looked out her kitchen window, saw the game Mark and Billy were playing, and felt a rush of horror. Running outside, she pleaded with her son and his friend to find some other, less dangerous way of amusing themselves.

Pole-vault practice, then, had to wait for Bill Olson, Sr. to come home. Billy's dad was a man who had always held athletic pursuit

*in high regard. Gently he persuaded his wife to let the practices
continue, assuring her there was little chance of her son getting hurt
falling from an altitude of approximately four and one-half feet.
After all, he reasoned, Billy was finally showing some interest in
athletics, and that was an interest to be encouraged.*

*For several days the neighborhood enthusiasm for the new sport
ran high. In fact, the youngsters quickly saw the need for a more
sophisticated landing pit and set about to dig a sizable hole in the
Olson backyard. They turned dirt repeatedly to assure themselves
softer landings after clearing the celestial heights they sought.*

*The damage done to the well-kept Olson yard, however, came
dangerously close to ending a budding career. Neither of the Olson
elders was in any way pleased with the hoe-and-shovel damage the
youngsters had done. Mr. and Mrs. Olson demanded that the backyard be immediately restored to its original state.*

*For several days, then, it looked as if Billy's pole-vaulting career
had come to an abrupt end. Then, however, Eula Mae Olson, his
understanding grandmother, came to the rescue. Having heard the
problems the young athlete and his friends were facing, she suggested a solution. With Billy accompanying her, she drove to a
nearby used furniture store and purchased a second-hand mattress.
Though it had clearly seen better days, it was viewed by the frustrated young vaulters as a top-of-the-line landing pit.*

Soon workouts were underway again.

*In time, Billy's confidence grew to a point where he sought new
challenges with the pole. The concrete fence which surrounded the
Olson backyard was seven feet high. To be able to vault to the top of
it, he determined, would be a worthwhile goal. Again his mother
was rushing from the house to warn her son of the dangers he
seemed determined to flirt with. This time Billy's father agreed with
her. Athletic pursuits, he said, were fine, but he had no intention of
making a trip to the emergency room. Vault onto grandmother's
mattress or forget it, Billy was told.*

*Though the fence offered a greater challenge, Billy satisfied him-
self with the more orthodox approach to pole vaulting for another
week or so. But then a sudden summer rain ruined his landing pit.
By the time the mattress had dried it was harder than the bare
ground.*

Thereafter the fickle interest of youth had turned to another direction. Pole vaulting was no longer fun. The prized bamboo pole was no longer of interest. Such, it seemed, was always the case with young Billy Olson. Few things held his interest for long. Particularly athletics.

If there is a city anywhere in the country that takes its sports more seriously than does my hometown, Abilene, Texas, I'm not aware of it. A long and rich athletic tradition existed long before I was born, and it has continued nonstop. In fact, one has to look pretty hard to find anyone of the 100,000 people who call Abilene home who doesn't follow the athletic accomplishments of the three colleges—Abilene Christian University (formerly Abilene Christian College), Hardin-Simmons University, and McMurry College—and the two high schools—Abilene High and Cooper High.

The tradition has deep roots. It is not at all unusual to see a youngster playing on a team on which his father had starred years before. Not only does the local newspaper, the *Abilene Reporter-News,* devote great amounts of space to the competitions of the colleges and high schools; it even sends writers out to cover junior-high-school football games. In the summer months, results of Little League baseball and summer track meets can be found in each morning's edition. Which is to say athletics is a vital part of the lifestyle in Abilene.

No matter where I go today, I can count on running into someone eager to express his knowledge of the West Texas town where I grew up. He doesn't mention trade or commerce or the rolling prairies and dust storms. Instead, he'll recite the accomplishments of the great athletes and teams that established remarkable records. For instance, Abilene High School, my alma mater, won three state football championships in a row back in the mid-'50s and boasted a national winning-streak record of 49 straight. *Time* magazine even visited to tell the rest of the world of the amazing number of victories. Six times, beginning in 1924, Abilene High has won the state track-and-field title. And there have been a couple of state baseball championships along the way as well.

Abilene Cooper, the newer of the two high schools, has also won state championships and produced a long line of outstanding athletes. A few years ago Jack Mildren, who quarterbacked the team to the state finals, was considered the top high-school player in the nation. So heated was the college recruiting for his services that *Sports Illustrated* chronicled the event in a lengthy article.

Though relatively small in enrollment, the three colleges have also enjoyed nationwide reputations. At the 1956 Olympic Games in Melbourne, Abilene Christian's Bobby Morrow won three gold medals, winning the 100-meters, the 200-meters, and anchored the winning United States four-by-100-meter relay. In 1960, another ACC student, Earl Young, won a gold medal as a member of the U.S. four-by-1600-meter relay and was a finalist in the 400-meter dash.

Teams and individuals from McMurry and Hardin-Simmons have also regularly enjoyed success on the national level.

In recent years you could find athletes who called Abilene home playing in the National Football League and on major-league baseball teams. Others have gone on to become outstanding college athletes and highly respected coaches.

I do this bit of hometown bragging to make a point—to emphasize the atmosphere of the city where I was born and still reside. Abilene is a community that holds strongly to its basic beliefs. Though progress has visited us, there is still a sense of the old-fashioned values. Abilene is God-fearing and hard-working. It owns a kind of community loyalty that seems to have been forgotten by many of the larger cities I have had the opportunity to visit.

Abilene has, by all measures, an ideal climate in which to grow and mature. It is also a place where some degree of ability in athletics gives one a natural avenue to acceptance, regardless of color, background, or bank account.

On the other hand, if you're not blessed with some athletic talent, it can be difficult. Quite frankly, one of the major pastimes of many adults is applauding the most recent accomplishment of their children. More often than not, that praise is for some touchdown scored or footrace won.

As a kid, I was a galloping failure at just about every athletic activity I tried. As a result, I never really enjoyed sports. When you're already in junior high and still a 90-pound weakling, it is rather difficult to even dream of football heroics. I lacked the height and coordination to do well at basketball. And, though I was careful never to give her the opportunity, my older sister Debbie could probably have outrun me. I did hit pretty well and played a relatively solid first base for the Go-Jets in Little League. But baseball just didn't interest me.

Which is to say I was a constant source of concern—and disappointment—to my father. It was clear to me that he badly wanted me to be an athlete, to find a sport to which I could really devote my energies and attention. That I didn't, I'm certain, troubled him a great deal. Not that he ever actually said so, but I felt it strongly and with a discomfort I didn't hide very well. I reacted to his urging and encouragement by rebelling. To add salt to the wounds he was already feeling, I did miserably in school, let my hair grow to shoulder length, and made a concerted effort to seek out friends who gained little or no approval from my parents.

I suppose I should point out that I was not a complete athletic wash-out during my elementary-school days. At some of the intraschool competitions we had what were called chinning relays— four guys from each school who chinned as many times as they could. The team with the greatest collective number won.

At the risk of sounding boastful, I'll have to say I was one chinning fool. I could chin all day, probably because I was so light and skinny. No one ever beat me. If chinning was an Olympic sport, I'd already have a gold medal.

I guess when you're the father of a kid who isn't good at anything but chinning, you learn to take what you can get. It seemed that, whenever someone came over to visit, not much time would pass before Dad had mentioned my chinning ability and hurried everyone into the backyard for a demonstration. Frankly, it became a little embarrassing, Dad counting as I huffed and puffed away, showing how many chin-ups I could do.

Visitors always expressed approval. But I have to believe they would have been far more impressed if I'd scored the winning basket or run for a much-needed touchdown at one of the games they regularly attended.

At the time I felt my father's constant pressure on me to find my athletic niche was nothing more than his own private wish to have me become something he once was. As a high-school student he had been an outstanding football and tennis player. While in the Marines he had won the intraservice tennis championship. And he was an enthusiastic weight lifter.

My dad has always been a fierce competitor and a man who gives the outward impression of being tough and demanding. Though he seldom talks about it, I'm told that during his days on the Abilene police force he was considered one of the toughest cops in town.

Once, while investigating an accident, Dad and his partner were involved in a chase and were run off the road by the person they were attempting to apprehend. Later, the same man, hiding in some bushes, shot Dad with a .22 pistol. The bullet hit him on the bridge of the nose, causing the loss of sight in his right eye.

The only reason he stayed in the hospital as long as he did, the story goes, was because of his attraction to one of the nurses who looked in on him from time to time.

Later that nurse became Mrs. Bill Olson. Dad likes to joke that he had to give up sight in one eye to find the right woman to marry.

Jay Hatcher, now a member of the Abilene Police Department, grew up with Billy. Together, they attended Lincoln Junior High School.

"When you got to junior high," Hatcher says, "it was expected of you to try out for football. If you didn't, you were pretty much a nobody. So Billy started out in football like the rest of us. But he was so light—at 5'6" he couldn't have weighed 90 pounds soaking wet. He was unbelievably skinny. I don't remember him ever getting in a game. In fact, I don't think he ever got off the last string. There's just no place on a football team, even a junior-high team, for someone built like he was.

"He didn't even try basketball, but did come out for the track team for reasons I'll never understand. There wasn't the slightest thing for which he had an ounce of God-given ability. He was skinny, weak, and slow—which is about the worst combination an athlete can be burdened with. To be honest, I wondered at the time why he bothered.

"But he had a great deal of desire and wasn't afraid of anything. I

think that's why, after considering all the events a track athlete can
try, he told the coach he wanted to try pole vaulting.

"He wasn't much good at it back then, but at least he had the
courage to try it. Most who did couldn't even get off the ground. The
whole idea of getting up in the air on the end of a pole, then free-
falling, bothered me. I tried it once, just for kicks, and found out
right away that it wasn't for me.

"But Billy stayed with it. We would stand around and watch him
try to vault. Which he didn't mind at all. You have to understand
there has always been a little bit of the show-off in Billy. To be
honest, though, if we hadn't liked him so much, we'd have been
laughing at him. I mean, here was a guy who had neither the speed
nor the strength to do what he was trying to do. Frankly, he was
pretty awful."

I may have been little and slow, but I wasn't dumb. When the
coach called for volunteers for the football team the next season, I
went to him and offered my services as a manager. I figured I
would play just about as much in that capacity and, as a bonus,
wouldn't have to get my brains knocked out in practice every day.
Needless to say, the coach didn't mourn the loss of a budding star.

In truth, I was a frustrated athlete. I knew I had no future in
football, yet I wanted to be a part of the group, to be accepted, to
make some sort of contribution.

It wasn't an attitude my father understood. He was light years
removed from happy when he learned that I was passing out towels
instead of practicing blocking and tackling. When I told him of my
decision, he angrily lectured me on the importance of making
something of myself, pointing out that being a manager was hardly the way to do so.

It frustrated him greatly, I think, that the competitive fires
which burned inside him didn't seem to be ignited in me. I knew he
was disappointed and I wanted in the worst way to do something
that would gain his approval. But I was at a loss to figure out what
avenue to take.

A few silent days later he showed up one afternoon at the practice field and told me he was taking me out of football. It was an
embarrassing scene. He said if all I was going to do was be a

manager I should get into some other sport. He told me I was to go out for the tennis team the next day.

He even bought me a nice racquet and enrolled me in tennis lessons that I was supposed to take after school. But, instead of going to the lessons, I just took my time walking home from school every afternoon.

For a while Dad went out and hit some balls with me, trying to help me in any way he could. And, actually, I was doing okay at it, despite skipping the lessons. But I just couldn't generate any sincere interest in the sport.

By the end of the school year the whole tennis idea had fizzled out. Dad found out I wasn't taking the lessons and he quit practicing with me.

After that, he quit pushing me. I think he gave up on me then and resigned himself to the fact I was never going to amount to much.

He never said much about it, and never really gave me a hard time about my failures and lack of interest. But, looking back, I know it was difficult for him to deal with.

Being Billy Olson's father wasn't exactly the greatest job in the world back then.

Bill Olson, Sr., now an Abilene bail bondsman, admits there were frustrating times when his son was younger, but he never came close to giving up on him.

"Maybe I just got a little smarter as time went on," he says. "At some point I guess I realized that the only thing to do was let nature take its course, let him find his own way.

"We had our difficult times, but probably nothing most fathers and sons don't go through. I think there's an age when most kids have a difficult time relating to their parents. And there's an age when parents' expectations of their children are too great. We all get in a hurry to see how they're going to turn out.

"The thing that puzzled me most about Billy when he was younger was that he had such a competitive spirit but didn't seem to take advantage of it. He had this drive that you don't see in many people but didn't seem really interested in sports.

"I remember one night he came into the bedroom and asked me

how many push-ups I could do. I told him I could probably do 50 or so. He dropped down to the floor right there and started doing push-ups. I don't remember how many he did, but he kept going until I was afraid he was going to hurt himself. I kept telling him that was enough—to stop. But he kept right on.

"Back when he was younger, I wanted him to get involved in some kind of sport—like tennis, for instance—that he could enjoy for a lifetime. I never really encouraged his going out for football because he was so small. In fact, I was worried that he might get hurt. But, yes, I felt it was important that he involve himself in some kind of physical pursuit.

"It wasn't that I wanted him to grow up to be a superstar athlete so I could run around town bragging. I just wanted him to give sports a chance.

"To show you how much I know, I never encouraged his pole vaulting that much in the early days. I never dreamed it would benefit him the way it has.

"In a way, it's ironic. I tried to point him in a number of athletic directions with little or no success. I coached his Little League team, I played tennis with him, we hit golf balls together. But none of it really interested him. He found pole vaulting on his own, and has pursued it with an almost fanatical zeal.

"That, I think, is the way it has to be if it is to work. Billy and I both learned that the hard way, I suppose.

"But we learned it. That's the important thing."

My junior-high athletic career ended with a whimper. I had tried pole vaulting again in the ninth grade with little success. I cleared something like 10 feet, 6 inches before developing a knee problem that forced me to give it up.

At the time I felt it was just as well. Jumping 10-6 wasn't going to win any blue ribbons anyway.

I wasn't setting any academic records, either. My C average didn't win me much applause at home, and the thought of advancing on to high school, where things were going to get tougher, didn't exactly have me counting the days until time to enroll.

I was also fast running out of sports to try. Dad, meanwhile, had exhausted all the tricks he knew to motivate me. For instance, while trying to interest me in tennis, he had taped a fifty-dollar check to the door of the refrigerator in the kitchen. It was mine, he told me, if I ever beat him at tennis. (I told you he was competitive.) It stayed there for quite some time after I quit playing. Then one day I went to get a glass of milk and noticed it was no longer there.

It was my grandmother—not the one who had purchased the mattress for my backyard vaulting pit, but my other grandmother, Pearl Wood—who suggested I give golf a try. Herself a club champion who probably could have made it on the professional women's tour had she been so inclined, she invited me to play with her and my grandfather, H. M. Wood. When I would visit them at their home in Granbury, Texas, they would have me up at five in the morning, hitting practice balls at a nearby golf course.

In short order I had my own set of golf clubs, purchased by my never-say-die father. And I was getting up early in Abilene, too, to go out and hit a bag of shag balls—working on my swing, experimenting with the various clubs. Dad and I even began to play some together.

Finally, I decided, I had found a sport I was comfortable with. It demanded no great strength or speed afoot and afforded none of the pressures team sports presented. Golf, I decided, would be the sport I would pursue in high school.

I hardly set the world on fire, but I really enjoyed the game. By the time I entered Abilene High School I was good enough to make the team, but not the traveling squad. Which is to say I got to practice a lot but never got the chance to compete in tournaments. That reward was reserved for the top five or six players on the team.

In truth it wasn't something that bothered me a great deal. Arnold Palmer and Jack Nicklaus were safe. I was playing for the fun of it. Making trips with the team seemed far less important to me than hanging around with my friends, listening to rock music, drinking a little beer on Saturday nights, smoking occasional cigarettes, and having a good time.

Golf didn't demand a great deal of strict training, and I took full advantage of the fact.

I had, with what seemed to me very little effort, developed into a dyed-in-the-wool rebel without a cause. I didn't concern myself with anything more serious than the price of admission to the movies and a date for the weekend. At home, I was getting a hard time over the length of my hair, my refusal to accompany the rest of the family to church on Sundays, the quality of friends I had cultivated, and the grades I was making. By the time I was a sophomore I was ringing all the negative bells.

I'm certainly no psychologist, but as I look back, I think perhaps the happy-go-lucky, never-take-anything-too-seriously Billy Olson was just a kid who hadn't found anything to demand his attention. I wasn't running away from anything, nor did I feel down on myself. But I was rebellious. And I'm not certain why.

I saw myself in my dad's eyes as being something of a bum. And I didn't like it. But I didn't know what to do to begin erasing that image.

In the summer following my sophomore year, one of my best friends, Benny Muzachenko, spent a lot of afternoons out at the Abilene Christian College track, practicing pole vaulting. As a sophomore he had been the best vaulter in Abilene High and was getting ready to compete in a series of summer meets sponsored by the city recreation departments in West Texas.

Quite often I would go out to the track with him to watch him vault, catch his pole for him, help him get his step down, things like that. It was something to do.

Another friend, James Barefoot, would usually go with us. We'd run a little, mess around on the high-jump pit, lie around in the sun. Benny was the only one out there with any real purpose.

Still, I spent quite a bit of time watching him, offering suggestions, giving him a hard time when he missed a jump, and cheering him on when he vaulted well. He was dead serious about what he was doing and the rest of us were just goofing off. And, while I kidded him a lot, I really admired the attitude he had toward what he was doing. Obviously he enjoyed pole vaulting and wanted to be as good as he possibly could. It was an attitude I really had very little experience with at the time.

One afternoon he put the standards up to 12-6. After warming up he tried the height several times but couldn't get over. Clearly, he was getting frustrated. And I wasn't helping matters any by running my mouth. I said, "Anybody ought to be able to get over 12-6"—or something to that effect.

Benny finally had enough of my wise-guy act and suggested that, if I knew so much about the fine art of pole vaulting, maybe I should try making the height myself.

Suddenly I was in one of those put-your-money-where-your-mouth-is situations. I borrowed his pole, did a couple of runs down the runway to warm up, took a jump—and cleared the bar with an ease that surprised even me.

For the rest of the afternoon he and I vaulted together, coaching each other and offering suggestions far more serious than those I'd been giving him earlier in the afternoon.

To his frustration—and my surprise—I was beating him immediately. It seemed natural to me. Not that we were threatening any records, but he *was* considered the top vaulter in school.

For the remainder of the summer I practiced with him on occasion. It was fun. But I hardly considered myself a candidate for the track team. At six feet and 125 pounds, I felt the best place for me was on the golf course, practicing for tournaments I would never enter.

Evidently Benny felt differently.

When it came time to start school the following September, I was standing in the line for those wishing to sign up for golf when Pat Aguilar, the Abilene High track coach, tapped me on the shoulder. "Billy," he said, "unless you're really interested in playing golf this year, I'd like for you to come out for track. I hear you have possibilities as a pole vaulter."

I'm reminded of a story I read not long ago about how Roger Staubach, the outstanding Dallas Cowboys quarterback, came to choose his position when he was a kid first starting out in football. He said that when he reported to the gym where all the prospective football players were gathered, the coach told everyone to get in lines according to the positions they wanted to try out for. Roger had made up his mind that he wanted to be an end. But when he went to the appropriate line he saw it was one of the longest there. He stepped back, looked around, and realized the line for quarterback was the shortest. So he moved over to that line.

Makes you believe there's something to the business of fate.

I thought about Coach Aguilar's suggestion for a minute, then walked away from my not-so-hot golf career and into the line of athletes registering for track and field. Once again, I was quitting a sport.

But I was returning to one as well. Maybe, just maybe, I could become a pole vaulter after all.

Evidently Benny Muzechenko and James Barefoot, who had suggested the coach talk to me, thought so. In the days to come I would begin to realize just how much I owed them—particularly Benny. The year before he had been number one on the team. Yet he was unselfish enough to encourage me to try out for the team, fully aware that I might be able to beat him as I had done several times during the summer.

James Barefoot, a life-long friend of Billy's, remembers those days when the young Olson was far more interested in having a good time than anything else—when the structure and dedication of athletic pursuit were not a part of his lifestyle.

"We got in our share of trouble," he says, "and did some things none of us will probably ever talk about to anyone else. But we weren't all that bad. I don't think any of us were headed toward a life of crime or anything like that.

"So, I'm not saying that if Billy hadn't taken up pole vaulting he would have gone off the cliff. But it did help him, change him. His priorities were rearranged once he really got into it and began to realize he could be good, could excel at it.

"And, yes, over the years he's changed a great deal. But, believe me, it didn't happen all at once. . . ."

3

High-School Champion

IN THE 16 MAY 1976 EDITION of the Austin American Statesman, the following story, written by sportswriter Bud Kennedy, appeared:

> A state high school track meet usually looks like a running back convention. Thus Abilene's Billy Olson fit in as well as Truman Capote might have Saturday afternoon.
>
> Olson is—well, he looks a bit underfed. At 5-11, 130 pounds, with veins bulging in his lean legs, cigarette stains on his teeth, and long blond locks, he wouldn't remind anyone of Charles Atlas.
>
> But when Olson slipped over the bar at 15-9 in the Class AAAA pole vault, he slipped into the state meet records, and slipped the Eagles a state championship.

The review was, to put it mildly, not greeted warmly in the Olson household. Billy's father, irate over the suggestion that his son's teeth were stained by excess cigarette smoking, wrote an angry letter to the sports editor of the Austin paper, expressing his complaint and pointing out that most of the youngsters from Abilene have some discoloration of their teeth because of high amounts of gypsum in the water of the region.

Soon thereafter a letter arrived at the Olson's Lexington Street address, carrying with it a profuse apology from the Austin paper's sports editor. Among other things, he assured the elder Olson that the writing days of young Bud Kennedy were over.

Indeed, the aspiring journalist (who is today regarded as one of the top sports-department administrators in the state, working as an editor for the Fort Worth Star-Telegram*) was reassigned to office duty—writing headlines, selecting photographs for the next day's edition, and editing copy.*

"I made a serious mistake," Kennedy remembers, "and I paid the price. That's probably the way it should have been. I was just trying too hard to be colorful in my description of Billy. Rather than come right out and ask him if the stains on his teeth were the result of his smoking, I just assumed they were. The only real excuse I can come up with is the fact I was young then, just getting started in the business. I was trying too hard to impress people that I was a real hotshot reporter.

"You know, looking back on it, the thing I regret most is that I might have hurt Billy. He was a very modest, likable youngster. It's just that I was so taken aback by his physical appearance. In Texas, winning a state championship is a big deal—and he simply didn't look like someone who might lead his team to a state title and set a record while doing it."

Kennedy has, like virtually every sportswriter in Texas, followed Olson's record-breaking career closely. "I've seen him vault a number of times since he was a senior in high school," he says, "and I'm very impressed with what he's accomplished.

"In fact, I consider myself one of his biggest fans. A couple of times at meets I've thought about going up to him and apologizing for the story I wrote."

The truth of the matter is, that writer came a lot closer to hitting the nail on the head than some I've encountered. Looking back, I know I hadn't smoked enough to stain my teeth—but I did smoke. And I drank more than my share of beer and stayed out too late too often. And did several other things my father wouldn't have approved of.

There was a time in my life when I felt it was necessary to do crazy things to impress my friends. If it meant smoking and drinking and refusing to accompany the rest of the family to church on Sunday mornings, that was okay with me. It was the thing to do if you were to be judged cool by your peers.

As I look back on some old photographs taken during my high-school days, I know I wasn't exactly a candidate for Most Handsome.

So, no harm done, Mr. Kennedy.

Until my junior year in high school I can't honestly say I had made a full-fledged attempt to succeed at anything. And, frankly, the only logical reason I can come up with for staying with pole vaulting that year was the fact that I was fairly good at it from the very beginning.

I was still painfully slow and certainly hadn't begun to bulge with muscles. But it all seemed to come naturally. I had pretty good coordination—which is essential—and I wasn't afraid of the event. Also, it was about the best way in athletics to show off.

My first real competition was in the San Angelo Relays that spring. I vaulted 13 feet, 6 inches to win second place. Winning that silver medal was a special feeling. And I was pretty confident that I would soon be winning some gold ones.

Those ideas went by the wayside the next week in a meet in Snyder. On my first attempt I was well into the vault when my pole broke in four pieces. It sounded like someone had fired a pistol. Fortunately, I landed in the pit, but I was shaken by the experience. I doubt if I would have vaulted again that day, even if I had had the luxury of another pole.

On the bus ride home my confidence was at a low ebb. But then Coach Pat Aguilar sat down by me and began telling me I really had a future. He admitted that he wasn't the world's foremost expert on pole vaulting. But he said that he would give me the benefit of what knowledge he had, and that we could learn together. Then he really surprised me, saying that he was going to order not one, but two new poles first thing Monday morning.

You might think that a vaulter can compete just as well with one pole as another. After all, just about every high-school vaulter uses a 14-foot fiberglass pole. But even those poles made by the same manufacturer are different. Each has a unique feel to it, a certain flexibility with which you're either comfortable or you're not.

For several weeks after the new poles came, my vaulting looked a great deal like it had back in those backyard days when I was playing around with a length of bamboo the Hallmarks' carpet came on. But Coach Aguilar stuck with me. I became discouraged and he encouraged me. I grew lazy and he got on me. I let my priorities get mixed up and he wore my rear end out.

One weekend we were competing in a meet in Hobbs, New Mexico on a weekend that a friend of mine named Mike Little and I had really important dates. Even before we left Abilene by bus I was reasonably certain that we wouldn't get back in time for my date.

So Mike and I devised a plan. He had a new car he loved to drive, so he suggested that he would drive to Hobbs and watch the meet, then I could come home with him instead of on the team bus. That, we felt, would save us the necessary time.

But as the meet went on, it became more and more obvious that even having a getaway car standing by wasn't going to get me home in time to keep my date. I sought Mike out in the stands and told him of my new plan:

The pole vault competition would probably take at least a couple of hours. The officials had indicated they would begin the vaulting at 12-6. What I would do, I explained to Mike, was miss three straight times at the opening height and eliminate myself from the competition. Then I could shower and we'd be on our way.

I made three miserable attempts at 12-6, put on a great show of anger and disappointment, and took off for Abilene. We were a little late, but our dates were waiting. All was well. Until I got home.

Coach Aguilar, more than a little upset over the fact that I had not ridden the bus home with the other members of the team (he wasn't aware that I had no-heighted intentionally), had called the house several times asking if my parents had heard from me. Needless to say, I got nothing resembling a hero's welcome when I returned home.

I knew full well that I would be getting licks from Coach Aguilar when I got to school Monday. To prepare for that eventuality, I put on as many pairs of underwear as I possibly could and still get my jeans on. They cushioned the blows some, but not to the point I can't remember them well to this very day. Coach Aguilar could swing a pretty mean paddle.

Pat Aguilar insists that Billy was no more a disciplinary problem than most high-school boys. "In fact," he says, "Billy was a lot less trouble than some I had. All the demands and sacrifices of athletics were pretty new to him when he first came out for the track team. He had to learn about them, just as he had to learn the techniques of pole vaulting.

"Our biggest confrontations were over his work habits. He would get lazy or discouraged now and then and I would have to get on him.

"I remember one afternoon I went down to the pole-vault pit to watch him for a while and he was looking terrible. Finally, in disgust, he said he was going in—wasn't going to practice any more that day.

"I asked him if he had warmed up properly before he started vaulting. He told me what he had done, admitting that he had skipped a number of things necessary to get his body loose and ready for vaulting. I told him that instead of going in he was going to start his workout all over.

"He didn't like that at all and said he wasn't going to do it. I told him, fine, go on in. But I said that, if he did, he should check his uniform in while he was in the dressing room, because I didn't want him back."

What makes the confrontation even more interesting was the fact that Billy's dad, who often came to watch his son practice, stood by listening to the conversation. His silence made it perfectly clear that he sided with the coach.

"One of the things that really helped Billy along," Aguilar says, "was the tremendous support he got from his family. There were people in town who thought Billy and his dad didn't much like each other—and at times both of them gave that impression—but there was never any doubt in my mind that there was a strong bond between them. Billy wanted to please his father. And his father wanted him to make something of himself. As far as I'm concerned, that's an unbeatable situation so far as father-son relationships go."

Today Pat Aguilar no longer coaches track. He is defensive coordinator of the El Paso (Texas) Austin High School football team. But he often thinks back to those days when he coached some of the finest schoolboy track teams in Texas history. He still has film of Billy Olson vaulting and occasionally gets it out and watches it.

"I'll be the first to admit that I didn't know much about pole vaulting. But I know enough to say that his technique wasn't much back then. And he was probably the slowest kid we had on the track team, including the shot-put and discus people. But he had some natural gymnastic ability, and he was absolutely fearless. Plus, even in his first year on the team, you could see that he had a special kind of inner determination that was going to get stronger and stronger.

"If I did make a contribution to Billy's success—and every coach likes to think he did help those he worked with—it was because I forced him to do his drills and taught him the importance of discipline."

What Coach Aguilar didn't point out was that I must have seemed like a very slow learner. Even while I was enjoying pole vaulting and steadily improving at it, I wasn't ready to make the necessary full-fledged commitment. I wanted to have my carefree fun-and-games and be a champion athlete at the same time.

Eventually, I would learn that's impossible.

As the season went on, however, I did feel a sense of accomplishment, a sense that I was doing something positive and worthwhile. On the other hand, I guess I was a little hesitant to take it seriously, for fear that it might not be a lasting thing.

After a while, though, several of my friends began trying to convince me that it was time I really dedicated myself to athletics. We would go out and have a few beers, and someone would say to me, "Hey, you shouldn't be doing this. You've got to keep yourself in shape. You've got meets to think about, your senior season to get ready for, a scholarship to shoot for."

What they said made sense, I had to admit. Running around, acting crazy wasn't getting me anywhere. I began to think maybe they were right. And toward the end of my junior year I began to settle down and listen to some of the lectures on discipline that Coach Aguilar was always giving.

In truth, many of my buddies were more convinced of my abilities and bright future than I was. I was improving, but the fact remained that I wasn't even the best high-school pole vaulter in town.

Over at Abilene Cooper, Dave Flamming, a guy I respected greatly, was the number-one-ranked vaulter in the state. And, like me, he was only a junior.

At the district meet that spring, he cleared 14 feet, 9 inches to win. On the same day, I cleared a personal best of 13 feet, 9 inches—a foot lower than Dave—to get second place. Winning second did qualify me for the regional meet, which was an accomplishment, but getting beat by a foot in the pole vault is like losing a mile run by almost a lap.

If I was ever going to become the best vaulter in town, much less in the state of Texas, I had a great deal of ground to make up.

My father was more than eager to help. I had found out, in fact, that back when I had first expressed some interest in pole vaulting in junior high he had gone to Ricky Parris, an outstanding vaulter at McMurry College in Abilene, and asked if he could give me some pointers. Ricky, who would later become a good friend, had watched me briefly back then and told Dad there was very little he could do for me until I got a little stronger. I think it was his polite way of saying he didn't think I had much chance of ever being much of an athlete.

Later, during my junior and senior years in high school, Ricky was a great help to Dave Flamming and me. A couple of times a week we would go over to McMurry and he would work with us on technique. A state high-school champion from nearby Wylie High School, he had improved to become a 17-foot vaulter in college. Later, he would take a coaching job at one of the Abilene junior highs.

I don't think I've ever met anyone who knows more about the technical aspects of vaulting. He studied films constantly and taught me the importance of doing the same. He viewed the event as a science, breaking it down into minute parts. I think my exposure to his teaching during the early stages of my career helped me avoid some of the bad technical habits I could easily have picked up.

Winner of the NAIA (National Association of Intercollegiate Athletics) indoor and outdoor vaulting titles in his junior and senior years at McMurry, Ricky Parris is the one who made pole vaulting a featured event in Abilene track-and-field circles. His success inspired young vaulters throughout the public school system.

Even today, in fact, high school coaches from throughout West Texas bring their aspiring vaulters to attend clinics which Parris conducts.

"The first time I saw Billy trying to vault," Parris says, "he didn't look like much of an athlete. He was skinny and had very little strength. I remember telling his dad that he would simply need to get stronger and grow some before he would be able to do much in the way of athletics.

"I didn't see him again until he was a junior in high school. He didn't even look like the same kid. He had grown about six inches and his coordination had improved a great deal. He was still skinny, but he seemed stronger.

"We developed a pretty close relationship when he was in high school. We studied a lot of film of top vaulters, and either I was at Abilene High or he was out at McMurry almost every day. I got in touch with George Moore, an executive with Pacer poles, and talked him into sending me some poles, which I gave to Billy.

"It really makes me feel good to see him doing so well now, but I can't really take much credit for what he's done. I helped where I could back in his high-school days, but he did a lot of it on his own. And he had an excellent coach at Abilene Christian.

"Still, every now and then he'll call if something's going wrong and we'll get together to see if we can determine where the problem is. I've seen him vault so many times I can almost tell if there's something wrong just by listening to him run down the runway."

The Sunday after the district meet in my junior year, I told Dad that I was going to spend the afternoon vaulting out at Abilene Christian and asked if he would like to come along. We went by the high-school fieldhouse to pick up my pole, then planned to drive on out to ACU on the edge of town for my workout.

When we got to the fieldhouse, however, I found that Hector Soto, another vaulter on the team, had decided to do some weekend practice himself and had taken the pole I generally vaulted with. The only other one available was considerably heavier than the one I was used to. But, with no real alternative, I decided to give it a try. I could go back to working with the lighter one when regular practice resumed Monday after school.

Once at the Abilene Christian track, Dad helped me set up the vault standards and measured my steps on the runway. I warmed up and began experimenting with the new pole. Initially, it felt a bit cumbersome and hard to balance. But in time I was clearing heights close to what I had managed at the district meet. And it felt easy.

I decided to experiment further, raising my grip on the pole by a foot. After that something incredible happened.

Before the workout ended and we tied the pole to the side of the car to return it to the high school, I had cleared 15 feet! Thanks to the fact that Hector Soto had taken my regular pole and forced me to try vaulting with a heavier one, I had done something I wouldn't have believed I would be able to do in my lifetime.

I wanted in the worst way to tell someone. And I think Dad could have been easily pursuaded to purchase a billboard to advertise the breakthrough. But, as we drove home, he suggested I say nothing to anyone about it. The city meet was coming up in just a couple of days. "Don't tell 'em; show 'em," he said.

I couldn't wait for the Abilene High-Cooper High dual meet. That afternoon, with no one but my father to serve as witness, I gained a great deal of confidence. It was then I felt that eventually I just might become the best high-school vaulter in Abilene, Texas.

One has to have spent some time in West Texas to appreciate the winds that blow during the spring months. There are days when pole vaulting is practically impossible, for the simple reason that the wind blows the bar off before you ever get a chance to vault.

The city meet was held in just such conditions.

For the pole vault to be held, officials stood on ladders at each side of the bar, holding it in place until the vaulters were just about to go over. Then they would let go in case one of us knocked it off. In many areas of the country such procedure would be considered unorthodox, but in Abilene it was fairly common.

Dave Flamming, of course, was favored to win. Coach Aguilar, in fact, had been getting a lot of chiding from other coaches for a statement he had made to one of the local sportswriters. In an article dealing with the upcoming city meet, he had been quoted as saying, "Billy will win the pole vault if he has a good day."

Frankly, it was a rather illogical statement. After all, I had never come within a foot of Dave in competition. Coach Aguilar's optimism, I have to admit, was based on the fact that I had let him in on the secret Dad and I had promised to keep between us.

The competition quickly came down to a head-to-head battle between Dave and me. And I think he was a little surprised that I was staying with him for as long as I had. I cleared 14 feet on my first try at that height. Then, when the bar was moved up to 14-6, I again cleared.

The next stop was 14 feet, 9 inches, the height Dave had cleared to win the district meet. He made it on his first jump. I missed on my first attempt, then cleared it on the second.

Then the officials moved the bar to 15 feet—and a crowd gathered around the vaulting pit.

On my first attempt at 15 feet, I got over the bar but brushed it with my chest as I was coming down. Still, it stayed in place for several seconds before falling off. The judges huddled to determine whether I had knocked it off or whether the wind had blown it off after I had cleared it. After what seemed to me to be an eternal debate, they ruled that I had cleared it. The jump was good.

There are precious few times in my life that I've been happier. I wanted to celebrate, to run around the track yelling at the top of my voice—something, anything. But since Dave had three chances at the height, I pulled on my warmups and waited.

He missed on all three attempts and it was over. I was a 15-foot vaulter and the city champion—for a few minutes.

No sooner had the competition ended than Glenn Petty, the Cooper coach, approached the pole vault officials with a rule book in his hand. He showed them a rule which, if adhered to, would make my final vault a miss. Then Coach Aguilar got in on the discussion. A full-blown controversy was abrew.

As the officials tried to come to some kind of decision, Dave came over to me and extended his hand. "As far as I'm concerned," he said, "you cleared it. You won. Congratulations."

Shortly thereafter, I was the one extending congratulations. The officials reversed their earlier decision and ruled that my attempt at 15 feet had to be judged a miss. By having cleared 14 feet, 9 inches on his first jump, Dave was ruled the winner on fewer misses.

Strangely, I wasn't even that disappointed. I felt as if I had taken a giant step that day. In my own mind, I had cleared 15 feet. And I was certain I would be able to do it again in days to come.

The next day there was a lead story in the paper about the big "controversy." But accompanying the story was a picture of Dave Flamming and me taken after the judges' decision had been made. It showed us walking off, arms around each other's shoulders.

I think I like that picture about as well as any that has ever been taken of me. It said a lot, I think. I had long respected Dave Flamming. And on that day I think he gained respect for me. Our friendship grew from that time on.

And that, I've learned over the years, is one of the greatest byproducts of athletic competition. The records come and go, but the friendships one develops along the way are lasting ones.

The following week, at the regional meet in Lubbock, Dave cleared 15 feet and won. I was third, losing out on a trip to the state meet to a vaulter from Lubbock Coronado High School named Randy Clayball.

Dave went on to place second in the state meet, and Abilene High finished second to Galveston Ball in the battle for the Class AAAA team championship, losing by just two points. For several days after the season was over I had an empty feeling. I had carried it with me since the rest of my teammates had left for Austin and the state meet. Suddenly having failed to qualify, I didn't feel a part of the team. Maybe if I had qualified, I could have scored the additional points that would have allowed the Abilene Eagles to return home as state champions instead of runners-up.

I resolved that the next time around I would be among those going to Austin, to the state meet. Now I had a goal. And, while I probably didn't grasp the significance of it at the time, my life now had some direction. I knew what I wanted to accomplish, and was finally ready to commit all my efforts to doing it.

There are times when the best-laid plans get waylaid.

As my senior year got underway, I found myself counting the days until the opening of track season. During the winter I lifted weights to improve my strength (I still looked like a scarecrow, however, at 6-2 and 130 pounds) and worked at gymnastics to improve my coordination. And I ran more than I'd ever run, hoping to improve my speed.

Then, just as the season was about to begin, things fell apart. I was running sprints when I suddenly felt this sharp pain high in my right thigh. It ran all the way up to my lower stomach. I fell to the track and couldn't get up by myself.

Initially, I thought maybe I was having an attack of appendicitis.

Mom and Dad came up to the school to get me and took me to the doctor. After examining me he called my parents into his office and told them I had injured some muscles in my groin and lower abdomen and suggested that further strenuous athletic activity could have a negative effect on the muscles. He suggested that I forget about pole vaulting anymore that year.

I left his office feeling more depressed than I'd ever been in my life.

The following day, however, we were in the office of another doctor. His diagnosis was much the same. But he said that once the injury was completely healed it would probably be okay to try running some. And, if that felt okay, maybe I would be able to try vaulting sometime before the season ended.

It wasn't the most encouraging thing I'd ever heard, but there was hope in what he had to say. I set about to do everything I could to get myself well as soon as possible.

I took heat treatments, which seemed to help little, if at all. I sat in the whirlpool endlessly, but the pain remained. And I began to swim. Swimming didn't require much use of the muscles that were injured and I thought maybe it would help me stay in shape while I waited for the pain to go away.

Looking back, the swimming was probably the best therapy. In time I was able to do some jogging.

But by the time the team bus left for the first meet of the year, I was still unable to run and had to stay home. That was about all I could take.

I told Dad that the muscles were feeling much better and that I'd like to try to vault. He talked it over with my mother and they hesitantly agreed. Coach Aguilar said he would enter me in the next week's meet in Dallas but that it was to be nothing more than a test. He didn't want me running hard or vaulting during the week. Once at the meet I could warm up, see how I felt, and try vaulting if I didn't have any pain.

At that point I would have agreed to anything.

At the Dallas meet I felt reasonably good warming up. There was no pain, but I knew I was rusty and not likely to vault well. Still, I decided to wait until the bar had been raised to 13 feet before entering the competition.

I made it over on my first jump—I'm not sure how—but that was it. The pain came back so strongly that I felt sick at my stomach. I didn't try another jump.

But I felt I was getting better. Rather than telling anyone how sharp the pain had been, I shrugged it off, saying that I had felt a slight twinge and thought maybe if I gave it one more week's rest I'd be okay. Coach Aguilar agreed.

The following week I did all my practicing in the training room, getting rubdowns and sitting in the whirlpool.

The next weekend, thrilled to be competing but still not sure how I might do, I took a chance and passed until the bar was at 13 feet, 6 inches. I cleared it, despite the fact that I wasn't able to run very well. Then I tried 14 feet and didn't come close.

The pain wasn't nearly so distracting, however. My problem was that I just couldn't run well enough to get up the speed necessary to clear the height I was striving for.

A week later I cleared 13 feet at the Border Olympics in Laredo, but couldn't go higher. It was beginning to look as if my senior year was going to be a colossal washout.

Frankly, I was just about ready to give up. The frustration was maddening. I'd never been in a position of wanting to do something so badly and not being able to do it because of an injury. My patience, never one of my strong suits, wasn't holding out very well.

Then, at a meet at Abilene Christian, I managed to get over 14 feet. There was no pain, and I couldn't wait to tell the coach.

"If that's the case," he said, "and you can get an okay from the doctor and your parents, we'll get you back on a regular training schedule. You've made it up to 14 feet without even practicing. Frankly, I think that's pretty amazing. Now maybe we can see what you can do with some work."

The next week, at the Bluebonnet Relays in Brownwood, I cleared 15 feet for the first time in my life. I felt like I'd just won the Olympics. At the end of the competition I was more tired than usual, a sign that I was not in the shape I should be. I think probably I could have cleared 15-3, maybe higher, if I had been in condition.

And I planned to be in condition as quickly as possible. My confidence, which had all but disappeared during those early weeks of the season, was coming back.

At the Texas Relays in Austin the next weekend I learned another valuable lesson. I had worked harder than usual during the week and, when the vault competition opened, I missed my first two attempts at 13 feet, 6 inches. I missed badly, in fact, and was worried that I would be eliminated with a third miss at the height. Coach Aguilar came over and told me to pass on my last jump and wait until the bar got to 14 feet, 6 inches before jumping again.

I thought he had gone crazy. "Look," he said, "there's no reason for you to mess with lower heights like this anymore. You're a 15-foot vaulter now. Remember that. You shouldn't waste your energies clearing 13 feet anymore. Just wait and let the competition thin the other guys out. Then you go for it."

I waited, cleared 14-6 on my first jump, and won the meet.

By the time we had won the district and regional championships, there was a great deal of talk about our being the team to beat for the Class AAAA state championship. Our sprint relay was threatening to break the national high-school record, our mile relay was the best in the state, and our sprinters, Donnell Baldwin and Charles Green, had good chances of finishing high in the 100 and 200 meters. And, finally, I was ranked number one in the state in the pole vault.

The week before the state meet, however, things looked pretty dark. At a warmup meet in Lubbock, two of our sprinters suffered muscle pulls. That same week, Donnell Baldwin cut his hand badly, and there was some doubt whether he would be able to take a handoff in the mile relay.

Then, to further complicate things, Tony Fields, who ran the second leg on our sprint relay, pulled a muscle the week before the state meet.

Instead of going to Austin feeling unbeatable, we arrived wondering if we would be healthy enough even to make a legitimate run at the championship.

And I was wondering if I would even be allowed to compete. Early in the week before we were to make the trip, Coach Aguilar called me into his office and told me he wanted me to get a haircut before the week was out. I immediately told him I saw no need to.

Seeing that reasoning with me was not going to get him anywhere, he put it to me another way: get a haircut or don't bother to show up at the state meet. "We need leadership on this team," he told me, "and here you are running around looking like a hippie."

For the next couple of days I pondered the situation. How, I wondered, was shorter hair going to make me a better leader? What right did he have to tell me that he wouldn't allow me to compete if I didn't show up with my hair shorter?

I made up my mind not to have my hair cut. And to avoid further confrontation with Coach Aguilar, I skipped the next two days of practice. Since we were allowed to travel to the meet with our parents, I managed to avoid my coach until just before time for the pole-vault competition.

By that time, however, I had experienced a galloping case of cold feet. Having convinced myself that he was serious and just might not let me compete, I asked my mother to give me a haircut the night before the meet. I'm sure it wasn't cut as short as coach would have liked, but it was shorter.

When I saw him on the field just before the pole vault got underway, he only smiled and wished me luck. Nothing more was ever said about the length of my hair.

Few athletic events I'm aware of are more colorful and exciting than the Texas high-school track-and-field championships. Held annually in Memorial Stadium on the campus of the University of

Texas, they are the gathering point of the finest runners, jumpers, and throwers from every corner of the state. The competitions, which are broken down into classifications according to the enrollment of each school, go on for two days.

On Friday night the Class AAA meet provided one of the most incredible individual performances I've ever seen. Johnny Jones of Lampasas High School had been the talk of the state all spring, running times in the 100-yard dash that were phenomenal. In one meet at Round Rock, Texas, he had run that distance in 9.05 seconds—the fastest time anyone in the world had run that year.

Needless to say, a sizable crowd had turned out to see if he was as good as everyone had been hearing. He was. After easily winning the 100 and 220, he prepared to run the final leg on the Lampasas High mile relay.

A first-place finish would earn the Badgers the state championship, but when the baton finally got to Jones, Lampasas was in seventh place, 40 yards behind the leader. It appeared to be a hopeless situation.

But in the middle of the Memorial Stadium backstretch Jones began to make his move. The 15,000 spectators were mesmerized. The public address announcer began detailing his every step: "He has moved up to fifth . . . he's fourth . . . third. . . ."

Into the straightaway he still trailed the two leaders, but an amazing burst of speed down the homestretch propelled him past the final two runners, and he hit the tape five yards in front.

The crowd went wild, pouring out of the stands to offer congratulations.

A reporter cornered the Lampasas coach and asked him what his talented sprinter could possibly ever do that would surpass the incredible performance he'd just given. The coach, proudly holding the state championship trophy in his arms, smiled. "He's going to take a shot at making the United States's Olympic team this summer."

A few months later, Johnny Jones, now a standout wide receiver for the New York Jets, earned a place on the Olympic team and ran a leg on the United States' gold-medal-winning four-by-400 meter relay in Montreal.

Such are the heroes the state track meet produces.

The morning before we were to report to the stadium, Coach Aguilar sat in the hotel lobby, pencil in hand. What he did with the piece of paper in his lap was magic. Because of the injuries we had suffered he was forced to do some last-minute rearranging. There's no doubt in my mind that he won the meet for us that morning in the hotel.

He decided to have a junior, Anthony Washington, run in Tony Field's place on the sprint relay. Charles Green, who had worked out very little since pulling up in the 100 in Lubbock, would run both relays, but not the 200 meters. In his place for the 200 meters, Coach Aguilar would substitute Herman Reece, who had earned an alternate's role with a third-place finish in the regional meet.

Donnell Baldwin, Anthony Washington, Charles Green and Herman Reece didn't break the national record, but they won the sprint relay going away with a time of 40.6 seconds.

Baldwin was second in the 100, pushing Curtis Dickey of Bryan (now with the Baltimore Colts) to the wire. Herman Reece came through with points in the 220, getting sixth place. And the mile relay of Willie Stephens (an outstanding football player who later starred at Texas Tech and tried out with the Chicago Bears), Baldwin (who had subbed for the injured Fields), Green, and Jerry Spence placed third.

And I won the pole vault, setting a new state record of 15 feet, 9 inches.

Winning a state championship is, says Pat Aguilar, something everyone involved in high-school athletics dreams of. "For most," he says, "it is the highest level they'll ever reach in athletics. Throughout their lives it is a touchstone, a memory to treasure. Certainly it's something I look back on with fondness.

"We had some kids on that team who had been labeled wrong by some people in the community. When they were younger they had gotten in a little trouble—nothing serious—and had to fight against that as they grew up. Bad reputations are hard to overcome. But in my mind they certainly did it. They worked hard, they overcame a lot of adversity, and they ended up as champions.

"Take Billy, for instance. In his younger days he was pretty headstrong and didn't always listen to advice. But, then, maybe that's not all bad.

"If he'd listened to his doctor's advice he would never have won the state meet in his senior year."

4

Important Decisions
GOLDEN HILLS
COMMUNITY CHURCH

In the parking lot adjacent to Austin's Memorial Stadium, Billy Olson stood with his parents, savoring the victory he had just accomplished.

As they talked, Clyde Hart, coach of the Baylor University track team approached, hand extended. He wore a wide smile. "Billy," he said, "you were outstanding. You did everything we had talked about your doing. You kept your part of the bargain, now I want to keep mine. I'm ready to offer you a full scholarship to Baylor. We'd love to have you."

For the second time in a matter of hours the Olson family had just cause for celebration.

Until my senior year in high school, the idea of a college education had entered my mind only on those occasions when my parents mentioned its importance to me. Frankly, the idea of four more years of studying, classrooms, and carrying an armload of books around wasn't something that caused me a great deal of excitement.

But as my vaulting improved I knew I wanted to continue it, to pursue some private goals I had begun to formulate. I wanted to see just how good I could be. And to do that, to continue competing, I would have to go to college. I viewed it as the price I would have to pay—something of an academic-athletics trade-off.

Thus the idea of a scholarship became more and more important to me in my senior year. On one hand, it would help my parents a great deal for me to be able to attend college at no cost to them. And, quite honestly, to an athlete the offer of a full scholarship—room, board, books, tuition, fees—is one of the measures of success by which he is judged. I was still very much interested in impressing my peers.

Feeling pretty good about my athletic accomplishments, I sat back and waited for the offers to roll in. The avalanche of calls and letters I expected never materialized. It didn't take me too long to realize that the entire collegiate track-and-field community wasn't ready to break its neck to get the signature of Billy Olson on a scholarship agreement.

In the first place, I was a one-event athlete. Regardless of how high I might vault, how many meets I might win, I would be able to contribute only a few points toward a team championship. On the other hand, a talented sprinter might be able to pick up points in the 100- and 200-meter dashes, the relays, and maybe even the long jump. College coaches, with a limited number of scholarships at their disposal, concentrated on signing athletes who would be able to score a number of points.

In the second place, I wasn't exactly a household name outside my home state. When, in fact, the *Track & Field News* high-school All-America team was announced, the three pole vaulters selected were Bill Hartley, a 16-foot vaulter from Manahawkin, New Jersey, Tom Hintnaus of Redondo Beach, California, and Brian Kimball of Fort Wayne, Indiana.

I was very interested in the University of Texas because I had friends there. Frank Estes, who had attended Abilene Cooper, winning the state pole-vault championship in his senior year, was a sophomore at UT and had just won the Southwest Conference championship with a vault of 17 feet, 3 inches. And a couple of his teammates were vaulting over 16 feet.

Additionally, the assistant track coach at Texas was James Blackwood, an Abilene High graduate who had captained the state championship team in 1959. When I talked with him, however, he said he could only offer me a half scholarship.

Texas A&M, Southern Methodist, and the University of Houston indicated they were interested in my coming. Coach Bill Mc-Clure, who had been the track coach at Abilene Christian before leaving to take the same position at the University of South Carolina, recruited me.

My parents were sold on Baylor, however. Several times, I would later find out, Dad called Coach Hart to see if he was reserving one of his 14 scholarships for me. He, in turn, was honest and to the point. He told Dad that he felt I had potential but he wanted to wait until the season was over, to see how well I performed at the state meet.

True to his word, he made his final judgment that afternoon in Austin. A week later he traveled to Abilene, scholarship agreement in hand, and I officially became a Baylor Bear. James Barefoot was going with me. Throughout my senior year he had stayed close by, always eager to help me in any way he could. Just as soon as he completed his basketball season, for instance, he had begun reporting to track practice every afternoon, helping me get the vaulting standards set up, catching my pole during workouts, and generally offering encouragement. In a sense, he was my unofficial coach, in addition to being a close friend.

Long before graduation we had decided we wanted to go to college together. Coach Hart offered him a partial scholarship to come to Baylor as one of the team trainers, and we signed our scholarship agreements on the same day.

Shortly after the state meet I received the news that my vaulting season was not yet over. Coach Aguilar informed me that I had been invited to participate in a couple of national high-school meets against the top vaulters in the country. It was an honor to be asked, and it would provide me an opportunity to see just how I might fare against vaulters who had cleared greater heights than I had.

In my mind, I was certain I could make 16 feet. For me, that was the magic number. And the additional summer meets would provide me with an extended period of time to continue trying to reach my goal.

I was convinced the injury I had suffered before the season began had put me well behind schedule. Because I had been unable to train and compete properly during those first weeks of the season, I felt I had been playing catch-up all year. In places like Kansas,

California, and Chicago, I thought, I might get the opportunity to prove I was among the top vaulters in the United States.

So, while everyone else on the team took leave of athletics, going off to summer relaxation and part-time jobs, I continued my training. Being the state champion was nice, something I knew I would cherish for the rest of my life, but I realized I wanted more.

And I think Coach Aguilar realized it. He got together with my parents and me and outlined plans for my summer season. There were, he pointed out, several meets where I could face a level of competition I had never seen before: the United States Track and Field Federation meet in Wichita, Kansas, the Junior Nationals in Knoxville, Tennessee, and then the two national high-school meets which would be held in Chicago and Sacramento.

I had already been accepted by the directors of each meet, he explained. Now, he said, there were two orders of business to be taken care of: I would have to continue my training and be ready, and funds would have to be raised to finance the trips. I took care of the training while Coach Aguilar and my dad went to work on the fund-raising.

Vaulting in the high-school division at the USTFF meet in Wichita, I cleared 15 feet, 6 inches and was named to the USTFF high-school All-America team. Quite honestly, I was feeling pretty good about myself. Being selected as an All-American was something special and I was more confident than ever that I was going to reach my goal of 16 feet before the summer was over.

The following afternoon, however, I saw something that returned me to earth. Staying over an extra day to watch the remainder of the meet, I saw Earl Bell win the pole vault with a world-record leap of 18 feet, 7¼ inches. It was an incredible achievement, and I had to wonder if the day would ever come when I would even be in a position to attempt such a height.

Having taken a movie camera with me, I photographed Bell's record-setting vault. And in the days that followed I viewed it over and over, studying his form, marveling at his strength and poise. Someday, I thought, that's the kind of vaulter I want to be.

The next stop would be Knoxville, Tennessee, and the Junior National Championships, a meet for track-and-field athletes who had not yet reached their twentieth birthdays. There, I knew, I would face the nation's top high-school vaulter, Bill Hartley, who had vaulted 16 feet a number of times. And there was even more incentive. The top two finishers in each event would qualify for places on the United States team which would travel to Moscow later in the summer for a dual meet against the Russian junior team.

In an irony I would not appreciate until some time later, my trip to the Junior National Championships was financed by several supporters of the Abilene Christian University athletic program. Coach Don Hood, the ACU coach, had an outstanding 400-meter runner named Randy Baker who was also entered, so we traveled to the meet together.

Hood, in fact, had helped me a great deal throughout the summer, making the ACU facilities available to me for practices and offering advice as he watched me practice.

In truth, I may owe him my life.

At Knoxville, I was standing at the end of the pole-vault runway, waiting to make my first practice jump, when I heard a sudden roar from the crowd. Above it all, I recognized Hood's unique voice. (His vocal cords had been crushed in an auto accident while he was in college and when he talked it was as if gravel was rolling around in his throat.)

He was yelling at me to get down, to duck.

I had no idea what might be happening. Nonetheless, I jumped to one side—just as the hammer, a 16-pound iron ball attached to a chain, hit my pole. Clearly, one of the competitors in the hammer-throw event had not perfected his aim.

Needless to say, I was shaken by the episode. Coach Hood came down from the stands to see if I was okay and explained that the arc of the hammer had appeared to be on a direct course with my head when he had yelled. I may be hard-headed, but not enough to have survived the impact of a 16-pound iron ball falling out of the sky. I'm convinced someone—in addition to Don Hood—was looking after me at that moment.

After a while I calmed down and redirected my attention to the competition at hand. Fortunately, the hammer throw was completed before the pole vault officially got underway. But on my first jump I was presented with a lingering reminder of the near miss.

On my first attempt, I was almost to the top of my vault when I heard a sound that is all too familiar to vaulters. It sounded as if someone had fired a .22 pistol right in my ear. But the manner in which I was suddenly falling backward toward the pit told me immediately that my pole had snapped. The impact of the hammer had obviously weakened the fiberglass and, under the strain of the bend and my body weight, it had broken.

Any vaulter who tells you that breaking a pole is not a harrowing experience probably has never had one break on him. More athletes than I care to think about have suffered serious injury falling after their poles have broken. There you are, 15 or 16 feet up in the air, your feet above your head, and suddenly you're falling. If you're lucky, you land in the pit and aren't hit by the jagged end of the broken pole. If not, you've got troubles.

In my case there was good news and bad news. I managed to land in the pit. The bad news was that my concentration was lost—and I was forced to vault with a smaller, lighter pole I had brought but had hoped not to have to use.

By day's end, Hartley had cleared 16 feet and was headed for the Soviet Union, along with a vaulter from the University of Texas at El Paso named Tim Vahlstrom. I managed to tie for fourth place with a jump of 15 feet, 6 inches.

And was feeling lucky about getting out of Knoxville alive.

The following week the main order of business was to get another pole. With the help of friend Ricky Parris, I got in touch with George Moore, a man in Carson City, Nevada who makes what most vaulters consider the finest poles on the market. He said he would send me a new pole directly to Chicago.

For the next few days I worked out with a smaller, lighter pole, then flew to Chicago for the Chicago International Prep Track and Field Meet. The pole George Moore promised was waiting when I arrived. I was concerned to note that the case it had been shipped in was broken in several places. But when I took the pole out it appeared to be okay. Maybe, I thought, this is the one that would take me up to 16 feet.

No such luck. On my very first jump in the competition the pole broke. And, to further complicate matters, part of it fell and hit me on the elbow. Shaken by two straight weeks of broken poles and flirtations with serious injury, I failed to clear the opening height.

Discouraged, I watched as Tom Hintnaus, the vaulter from California who had been born in Brazil, cleared 16 feet, 1 inch and won. And the following week I would have to face him on his own turf. The Golden West Invitational was my last chance of the summer to achieve the goal I had set for myself.

I managed to scrounge another pole and went back to work. Despite the fact that I had been a serious competitor for only a couple of years, I had already learned one of the cardinal rules of pole vaulting: If you are to continue improving, you have to put yesterday's failures and frustrations aside as quickly as possible. If you spend too much time worrying about what went wrong the last time you vaulted, you're going to find yourself failing again the next time out.

Thus if a vaulter seems self-assured at times, there is good reason. Confidence is the basis on which he builds his career. Without it, he has no business in the arena.

I made my first trip to the West Coast telling myself I was going to end the summer on a grand note.

In warmups at the Golden West Invitational I was clearing 15 6 with ease. Several of the other vaulters, including Hintnaus, were amazed and wanted to know what I had been doing the previous week. I felt I had my competition concerned, on the run.

Anxious to take advantage of the hot streak I seemed to be on, I rushed my jumps. Entering the competition at 15 feet, I was well over the bar but hit it coming down. It was a pattern that would plague me all afternoon.

When the bar was raised to 15-6, I again cleared by a foot or more, but clipped the bar coming down. Three times. And I was out. It was the first time I had failed to clear at least 15-6 in some time.

I returned to Abilene having placed a disappointing fifth. As the plane lifted off from California, I was even more discouraged than I had been when the doctors told me I would not be able to compete my senior year. Having had the opportunity to compete against the best vaulters in my age group in the United States, I had hardly distinguished myself. And I wasn't exactly thrilled with the idea that the people I had faced and lost to in recent weeks were the same ones I would be facing throughout my collegiate career. The competition, I realized again, was going to get considerably tougher.

I was left with two options: I could resign myself to being a pretty good vaulter who earned his scholarship but was always a few inches short of making it to world-class level; or I could dedicate myself to working harder and improve to a point where I could compete with the Hartleys and Hintnauses of the world.

Despite the dark mood I found myself in that summer evening as I flew home, I already knew I really had but one choice. I was convinced my best days were still in the future. I had, after all, been vaulting seriously for only two years.

And I still had a lot to learn.

The largest Baptist university in the world, Baylor University is located on the banks of the Brazos River—a picture postcard campus in the quiet, peaceful city of Waco, Texas. The Christian tradition of the school has long been recognized throughout the United States, as have the outstanding academic and athletic programs.

As a freshman, newly turned eighteen, I was most interested in Baylor's athletic program.

At that stage in my life, quite honestly, my spiritual growth wasn't much to brag about. (I knew my parents hoped that would change in the environment I was entering.) And my interest in academics had but one purpose. To be eligible to compete in athletics, the Baylor administrators, like those at all colleges and universities, demand that you make passing grades. I considered scholarship one of the necessary evils of competing at the college level.

Despite the required attendance at chapel services, I was convinced that at Baylor I could have the good time I expected from college life.

Thus I left home for college, priorities jumbled, few plans laid. From an earlier visit, I knew the campus was pretty—and so were the girls. Aside from pole vaulting, those seemed to be the most important considerations.

In time I would realize I had gone to Baylor for all the wrong reasons.

Midway through the first semester I was looking for a way out. My grades were reasonably high and I had made some good friends, but I was still unhappy because I felt I was going backward instead of forward in my pole vaulting.

Coach Hart's philosophy was foreign to anything I had ever dealt with. While I was certain the only way to improve as a pole vaulter was constantly to vault, he insisted that the fall months be spent running cross-country and lifting weights. I had done little of either and was convinced it was all wrong for me to do so.

I came to dread the weekly two-mile time trials that were required of everyone on the team. I could see no real reason to be running two miles to prepare myself for the 100-foot sprint down the pole-vault runway. Running cross-country drained all the spring from my legs. In time, everyone on the team was kidding me about how poorly I ran the two-mile trials. While others were running ahead, trying to beat times they had posted in previous runs, I stayed back in the pack, set for my weekly battle with a high jumper named Bill Wimberley for next-to-last place. Generally he won.

Once, I made up my mind that I would not finish last—that I would put all the jokes about my lack of endurance to rest. I resolved to run right with Bill most of the way, then to out-sprint him at the end.

When we got within sight of the finish line, I began my kick, moving ahead of him, in pain but enjoying the knowledge that my string of last-place finishes was going to end.

Fifty yards from the finish line, however, Wimberley began gaining on me. And just a few yards from the finish he inched past me, shoving me into last place again. That was the last time I ever made even a legitimate effort.

It didn't seem to matter a great deal since I had already made up my mind that I was going to leave Baylor. I had called Coach Hood back in Abilene to tell him of my disappointments, certain that he would welcome the chance to have me as a member of his team at Abilene Christian. After all, he had seen me vault enough to know my capabilities. And on more than one occasion he had told me he strongly felt I had the ingredients necessary to become a world-class athlete.

But, rather than welcoming me with open arms, he urged me to give Baylor a chance, to stay in school there for at least a year. It wasn't what I had hoped to hear.

Coach Hood's advice was wasted on me. I knew it would be only a matter of time before I left Baylor. I had already convinced myself that if I remained there my chances of becoming the kind of pole vaulter I wanted to be were nil.

The only thing to resolve was the direction I would head once I actually left.

When I came home for the Christmas holidays, I knew I probably wasn't going to return for the second semester at Baylor. I kept trying to convince myself that I should stick it out through my freshman year, but the enthusiasm just wasn't there.

All of this is rather difficult to explain, except to say I was immature and suffered from a severe case of tunnel vision at the time. Basically, I was doing all right at Baylor. My grades were the best I had ever made, and everyone was nice to me. Clyde Hart, the track coach, was an outstanding man, both personally and professionally.

But the bottom line—the only line—was that I wasn't vaulting as I felt I should. Coach Hart repeatedly insisted to me that things would come around if I would simply have faith in the program he had outlined for me. All the running, he said, was to develop a base. Once the spring arrived and I began concentrating on vaulting techniques again it would all come back to me, he promised.

I simply didn't have the kind of patience or confidence he had.

During the Christmas break, James Barefoot came by to tell me he wasn't going back to Baylor. And that solved it for me.

I sat down with my parents, expressed my concerns to them, and told them I wanted to leave Baylor, return to Abilene and enroll at Abilene Christian. There was little doubt they were disappointed. Active members of the Baptist church, they were happy to have me attending a Baptist university. And I'm sure Dad had been eagerly looking forward to my first year of competition in the Southwest Conference.

But, after hearing me out, my parents offered little argument. All they wanted to know was what my plans were.

I told them I wanted to enroll at Abilene Christian and have Coach Hood work with me. Dad suggested I drop by his house for a visit before making my final decision.

Once again the man I had come to respect so highly during the summer months suggested that I remain at Baylor at least through my freshman year. He knew Clyde Hart well and spoke highly of his abilities as a coach. And he pointed out that Baylor was one of the finest Christian schools to be found anywhere.

He also pointed out the fact that if I were to transfer at mid-term I would not be eligible to compete with the ACU track team that spring. The clincher was that he had no scholarship available to offer me.

For a while I couldn't decide whether he simply wasn't interested in having me on his team or whether he was trying to resell me on Baylor University.

Finally, though, I think I convinced him that my mind was set against returning to Waco. "Do this," he said. "Go on back to Baylor after the holidays and talk with your coach. See if you can work things out. I hope you can. But, if not, we'll work out something here. You know how I feel about your abilities. I think you can be as good as you want to be. And that's what I want for you—whether it is at Baylor or Abilene Christian."

That was what I wanted to hear. I shook his hand, promised to think about my decision some more, and told him I would be in touch.

Next came the hard part.

As the Christmas holidays neared an end, I called Coach Hart to tell him I wasn't coming back. I could tell he was hurt and disappointed. Having shown faith in me, giving me a scholarship and working with me throughout the fall, he was surprised that I was planning to leave Baylor and enroll in another school.

In the next several days members of the Baylor track team called, each one trying to convince me I was making a mistake. It was a difficult time for me. I had developed some close friendships during the first semester and could not help but feel I was betraying people who were depending on me.

But I had not reached my decision hastily. Painful though it was, I felt I was doing the right thing. I had made a mistake and had to do what I felt was necessary to correct it. A couple of days later I drove to Waco, picked up my clothes and personal items from the dorm, and returned to Abilene.

Once again I was going to be living at home. For the remainder of my freshman year I would be attending college without benefit of the scholarship I had deemed such a status symbol. To regain one, I would have to work to prove myself again. And I would have to do it without the benefit of much competition, since the rules would not allow me to compete for Abilene Christian until the following season.

Baylor coach Clyde Hart, regarded as one of the finest track-and-field coaches in the Southwest, was perplexed by Billy's decision. He felt the young vaulter had not given his methods a proper chance. And he was convinced that Olson had not come to his mid-term decision without benefit of council.

He wrote a letter of protest to the president of Abilene Christian, suggesting that Billy had been actively recruited by Don Hood. He knew that Hood had accompanied Olson on several trips during the summer and that he had worked with him on the ACU campus during that time. It was then, Hart said, that the subtle recruiting had begun.

To further demonstrate his anger over the situation, Hart severed ties with the Abilene school, saying that the annual dual meets his team had enjoyed with ACU would be terminated.

"There's no question I was disappointed to learn that Billy wasn't going to come back to Baylor," Hart says. "I felt he had great potential and I was looking forward to helping him develop it. True, we had never had a great vaulter at Baylor before he came, but I felt Billy would be the one to begin a tradition. But he didn't understand my philosophy. He was still just a skinny kid when he came here, and his speed really hadn't developed. Those were the things I wanted to work on first: get him stronger by lifting weights and improve his running. He felt he needed to be vaulting every day.

"But that's all in the past. His reasons for leaving aren't that important anymore. And I'm one of his biggest fans today.

"Still, I fuss at him now and then when I see him. We sat together on a plane going to the Athletic Congress meet last year and I told him I continued to read quotes from him to the effect that he left Baylor because the school pole-vault record wasn't even as good as what he had done in high school. That was true then, but things have changed.

"The truth of the matter is, Billy probably made a better pole-vault coach out of me."

Today, in fact, Baylor vaulters are consistently among the best in collegiate circles. The Southwest Conference record is held by a Baylor athlete.

"You know," Hart says, "coaches don't get the opportunity to work with potential world-record holders and Olympic champions that often. For most, it is a once-in-a-lifetime thing. It's a selfish stance to take, but I guess that's one of the reasons I was disappointed when Billy decided to leave Baylor.

"Still, if he wins the gold medal in Los Angeles—as I think he can—I'll be cheering as loudly as anyone."

The honest truth of the matter is I'm a homebody—and I am comfortable with the fact. Looking back, I think one of the reasons I went to Baylor was to get away from home. That's a motivation for many 17- and 18-year-olds graduating from high school. It's your first chance to get out into the world on your own and live your life as you think you should.

As I think about it, I've never really aspired to move to some bigger city, to move into a faster lane. I've been fortunate to travel to virtually every major city in the world over the last several years—and I've never found anywhere I'd rather be than Abilene, Texas.

So, it was good to get back, to renew old friendships and be on familiar ground. Once the decision to leave Baylor was behind me and I had settled into the routine of student life at Abilene Christian, I felt a great deal of pressure was lifted from my shoulders.

And my confidence began improving. Coach Hood, aware of my concern over not being allowed to compete, assured me that there would be some meets in which I could participate as an unattached athlete. And, he said, there was the National Junior Championships to consider again. That, in essence, was the carrot he dangled in front of me that first year at ACU. It was the goal he urged me to set for myself.

If I had to describe the prototype of a pole-vaulting coach it would be difficult. He has to know something about running, gymnastics, aerodynamics—and it wouldn't hurt if he were an amateur psychologist on the side. I mean, how many people do you know who would willingly go out and ride a fiberglass pole 18 or 19 feet into the air, try to get over a slender bar suspended up there in the clouds, then hope they are fortunate enough to land in the pit and not on the ground or a concrete floor?

Coach Don Hood is all those things and more. And he is one of the few track-and-field coaches who doesn't label pole vaulters as screwballs. He talks more about the fact that all successful pole vaulters are fearless, willing to take risks.

But there is much more to it. As he would show me.

In high school, Coach Hood was himself a vaulter, coached by Virgil Jackson, who later gained fame as the coach of two-time Olympic decathlon champion Bob Mathias. Back in 1948 he vaulted something like 11 feet. And while he is quick to admit he lacked the ability to become a championship-caliber vaulter himself, he developed a fascination for the event that he has carried with him throughout his life.

Today he has developed into an outstanding coach in all areas of track and field. But it is the pole vault that is his favorite, his specialty. He studies films of the great vaulters, constantly searching for new techniques to teach his own athletes. He stays abreast of the latest development in poles, and he is eager to learn of new training procedures that might improve an athlete's strength, speed, and coordination. Which is to say he never misses a thing.

After watching me vault for a while and recognizing that I sometimes had difficulty planting the pole in the box properly, he suggested I pay a visit to the doctor and have my eyes checked. I did, and came away wearing glasses, which I'd evidently needed for years. In one afternoon's practice, then, he solved a problem I'd had for some time without knowing it.

Although he is easygoing, Coach Hood is a man who has his

priorities in order. A witnessing Christian, he puts God first in his life. Next comes his family, then his work. I think in years to come, after all this business of chasing world records and an Olympic gold medal are done, I will look back on my association with Don Hood and remember him for a lot of things. For instance, there will be no way to fully repay him for the hours he has spent working with me, helping me become the athlete I am today. Most important, he taught me something about priorities.

But more about that later.

It was good to be vaulting again. At an indoor meet at Lubbock Christian College in January, I managed to clear 15 feet, 6 inches wearing jogging shoes and vaulting on a basketball court.

Coach Hood told me he wasn't as concerned with the heights I was clearing as he was with my approach to the bar. My run, he said, was not as controlled as it should be. And, just as I had been told at Baylor, I needed to improve my upper-body strength with a weight-training program.

Soon I began gaining some weight, going from 135 to 145. By the time the rest of the team was preparing for the outdoor season, I was eager to get into competition. I wanted to see if the things I'd been working on were going to be as beneficial as Coach Hood had assured me they would be.

Competing in a meet on the ACU campus, wearing my workout uniform instead of the purple and white jersey of those eligible, I cleared 16 feet for the first time. Though my effort would earn no points for the team, I felt as if I were on my way. The barrier that had stood in my way for over a year was now broken down.

"You're just beginning," Coach Hood told me. "By the summer when the Junior Nationals roll around, you'll have long forgotten about clearing 16 feet. You'll be going a foot higher, at least."

In April I was back in Austin for the Texas Relays, stronger and faster than I had been the previous spring when I had been there for the state high-school meet.

This time, however, I was vaulting not against other Texas schoolboys, but against some of the best vaulters in the world. In the field was Earl Bell, whose world-record vault I had witnessed the previous summer in Wichita.

I was not at all disappointed to return home having placed only fourth. I had improved my personal best to 16-6 and spent most of the ride home talking with my coach about going 17.

A month later, competing in the Meet of Champions in Houston, I did. Then, in a special pole-vault competition at a junior college meet in Abilene, I managed the height again, defeating Frank Estes, the Southwest Conference champion I had long admired, for the first time.

Having cleared 17 feet for the second time with relative ease, I had the officials move the bar up to 17-4. It was a mistake. Off balance at the top of the jump, I came down completely out of control, missed the pit, and hit the ground. I lay there for a minute, stunned, wondering in my foggy state what I might have broken.

Every bone in my body hurt, but fortunately none were broken. Shaken by the experience, I decided 17-4 would have to wait for another day.

The quality that has carried all great pole vaulters to the top is consistency. There are a number of vaulters around the world with outstanding vaults to their credit, but they haven't done it with any degree of regularity. Vaulting well at championship-level heights was the goal Coach Hood said I should shoot for. I should go into every meet confident that I could clear 17 feet and work from there.

In theory it sounded great.

What I did after my near-tragic miss at 17-4 was go into a slump like I'd never experienced before. During practice I couldn't get over the bar to save my life. Suddenly I was, by my own definition, the worst 17-foot vaulter in America. And time was nearing for the Junior Nationals.

Going into the meet, I was favored simply because I had managed the best height of any of the other entrants. The next best vault was Tom Hintnaus's 16-9. Despite Coach Hood's lectures on positive thinking, I arrived at the competition with my confidence at a low ebb.

And I proved it on my first attempt at 16 feet. Missing badly, I made another of those landings that looked like something out of an old Three Stooges routine.

Thinking maybe my pole was the problem (vaulters, you understand, have an unending list of excuses when things are going poorly), I borrowed one from a high-school senior named Jeff Buckingham.

On my third and final attempt at 16 feet, I cleared. It wasn't the kind of vault they are ever likely to use on a training film, but it felt great to finally clear height again.

When the bar was moved up to 16-6, Hintnaus and Paul Pilla, a vaulter from Florisant Valley Community College in St. Louis, cleared on their first attempts. Again it took me three tries, but I finally made it.

Then the officials asked the three of us what height we would like to attempt next. For several minutes we argued. Pilla and I wanted the bar to go to 16-9; Hintnaus wanted it at 17 feet. Both the other vaulters were well ahead of me on fewer misses. If all of us failed to clear 17, I would wind up third and they would be on the U.S. team that would compete against the Russian Junior National team.

I wanted to be there as well. It had been the goal I had set for myself after returning to Abilene. I stood my ground. Finally, Hintnaus agreed. By a vote of two-to-one, we went to 16-9.

On my first attempt it was as if someone had flipped a switch. Suddenly I felt under control on my approach. My balance was good, my lift felt right, and I was over the bar easily. The slump and all the dejection in which I had wallowed for several weeks was gone. After struggling through the opening rounds of the competition, I felt momentum swinging in my favor. Finally, the pressure was on the other vaulters.

Hintnaus missed on his three attempts, leaving the berths on the U.S. team to Pilla and myself. Thereafter the bar was raised to 17 feet, and neither of us came close.

Pilla was declared the winner of the event on the basis of fewer misses, but we would share the new meet record. And we were teammates, getting ready to wear a U.S.A. uniform in international competition for the first time in our careers.

The U.S.-U.S.S.R. junior dual meet had been held in the Soviet Union the year before, thus it was the United States's turn to host the meet. Richmond, Virginia, was to be the site.

The idea of representing my country, of knowing I had survived stiff competition to be selected as one of two junior vaulters to participate in the meet, was thrilling beyond anything I'd ever experienced. (Junior, in track-and-field terms, is an athlete who has not yet reached his twentieth birthday.)

On the other hand, I saw precious little chance of winning. The two Soviet vaulters who would make the trip were already considered among the best in the world, regardless of age. Viktor Spasov had cleared 17 feet, 8 inches to establish a world junior record, and his teammate, Alexandr Krupskiy, wasn't far behind at 17-6.

I figured Paul Pilla and I would have a tough battle between us for the bronze medal.

Fully aware that I wasn't ready to jump in the 17-8 range of Spasov, I made up my mind to relax, not concern myself with the other vaulters, and just do the best I could. I decided I would concentrate on vaulting against Billy Olson rather than against the rest of the field.

To this day I well remember my first impression of the two Soviet vaulters. They were juniors in age only. Watching them in warmups, I marveled at their strength and power. I suddenly felt like the 90-pound weakling at the beach.

I sought Coach Hood out in the stands and sat with him for a moment. Neither of us said anything as we watched the Russians, grim-faced, go about their preliminary warmups. Finally, as I left to begin my preparation, my coach wished me luck.

I looked at him and grinned. "Coach," I said, "this looks like the mismatch of the century."

"Don't be so sure," he said. "Funny things happen in the pole vault, you know." Then he offered a final bit of advice. "Don't enter the competition at the first height. Keep them guessing for a while."

The vault officials gathered the four entrants and informed us that the competition would open at 15 feet, 6 inches. Only Pilla chose to begin at that height. It wasn't his day and he missed on three attempts. That put him out of the competition.

When the bar was raised to 16 feet, 1¾ inches, I was the first up and cleared with several inches to spare. As always, it was a relief to get that first successful jump behind me, and I settled in to watch the Russians do the same.

It was obvious to me that neither had been shaken by my clearing the opening height.

As I sat watching, I was mildly surprised when both Spasov and Krupskiy missed on their first attempts. When both knocked the bar off on their second try, I was puzzled.

Then, to my amazement, both failed on their third and final tries. The competition was over, and I was the only one who had cleared a height. With just one jump I had won a gold medal for the United States and defeated the world junior record holder in the process. For several moments it didn't sink in. I sat there, on a bench near the vault runway, unable to convince myself that the competition had been over and done with so quickly.

From behind me, however, I could hear the cheering begin as the public address announcer gave the results: "Winner of the pole vault . . . Billy Olson of the United States . . ."

I've never been happier. I whispered a prayer of thanks and clenched my fists to keep my emotions in check. I wanted to run, to shout, to let the joy I was feeling burst out. Instead, I sought out the Soviets and my teammate to shake hands. I knew I had been lucky and I told them so. For the first time all day, the two Russian athletes smiled.

The official in charge of the pole vault asked me if I would like to attempt another height and I asked that the bar be raised to 16 feet, 8¾ inches. I made one less-than-impressive attempt and called it quits. My concentration was gone. For once, height wasn't the most important thing to me. Winning was—and I had managed to do it in my first international meet.

Back at the motel that evening, neither Coach Hood nor I could unwind. We talked of the season that had just been completed, of the remarkable turn of events just hours earlier, and of the future. I was on target, he pointed out. He had said he had wanted me to vault 17 feet as a freshman and I had made it, twice.

The next year, he said, the goal would be 18 feet. Thereafter, he expected me to add 6 inches per year. His plan sounded ambitious, even to someone who was feeling he could clear the heights we were talking of without a pole.

Realizing that I was keyed up and not likely to sleep for some time, Coach Hood suggested we get away from the motel room. "You may be able to beat me at pole vaulting," he said, "but I bet before the night is over I can find something I can whip you at."

For the rest of the evening we sought out every manner of competition the city of Richmond had to offer. We bowled; played pinball; tried shuffleboard, ping-pong, and shot pool. It was four in the morning before he finally surrendered. I had beaten him at everything we could find.

"Okay," he said as we returned to the motel, "I'll stick to coaching. You convinced me."

Weary but still not sleepy, we sat talking some more, savoring the day neither of us wanted to end. Finally, though, my eyelids grew heavy and I lay in bed, half asleep, replaying one more time the winning vault I had made earlier in the day.

The next thing I remember was Coach Hood bounding out of bed and saying something about taking a swim. Out the door he ran, wearing only his underwear, his legs so white they seemed to glow in the dark.

A few minutes later he was back, wet and shivering. Forty-degree weather, he said, was not really suited for late night swims.

I laughed. "Coach, you're crazy."

"In my business," he replied, "it helps."

Then, for a moment, he got serious. "Billy," he said, "I've enjoyed some great moments during my years as a coach. But today, watching you win against the Russians, seeing you standing on the winner's stand—was the best feeling I've ever had. I just wanted you to know that."

And with that we both fell into a deep sleep.

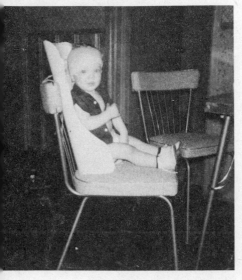

Left: The truth of the matter is I've been falling most of my life. The bandage on my head in this photo didn't come from pole vaulting, though. I was 10 months old at the time and had taken a swan dive off a chair. Below: That's me, third from the left on the back row, on my first Little League team. I was a pretty good hitter, not a bad first baseman, and even got to pitch on occasion. The coach on the right is my dad. Maybe that's why I got to pitch some.

I was really on cloud nine after this vault. It came at the state meet in Austin, Texas, during my senior year at Abilene High. Winning the state championship meant a great deal to me.

I doubt there is any school in the country that can boast of a more talented group of pole vaulters than Abilene Christian University had in 1982. From left to right that's Tim Bright, me, Brad Pursley, Dale Jenkins, and Bobby Williams. (Photo courtesy of Abilene Christian University.)

Opposite page and left: One of my major goals while a student at ACU was to collect eight National Intercollegiate Athletic Association championships by winning the indoor and outdoor pole-vault titles four years in a row. I made it, and it's a record unmatched in NAIA history. Here is the kind of jump that earned me one of those titles when the meet was held on the ACU campus. (Photos courtesy of ACU Sports Information Department.)

That's strain, not a smile, on my face as I clear 18 feet, 9 ½ inches to break the world indoor record for the third time in the 1982 season. This one came at the Jack-in-the-Box Invitational in San Diego. (Photo by Jeff Johnson, courtesy of *Track & Field News*.)

If you have any intentions of getting up there where the big boys vault, you've got to get a lot of bend into the pole on takeoff. And yes, they do break sometimes. (Photo by Charles Parker, courtesy of *Track & Field News*.)

Above: The bar is at 18-2½ and I'm over it pretty good, despite being bone-tired. This jump came at the 1983 *Dallas Times-Herald* Invitational, the night after I made 19 feet in Toronto. (Photo by Charles Parker, courtesy of *Track & Field News*.) Opposite page: When you're competing, it's nice to look up into the stands and find a friendly face. Here, at the 1984 *Dallas Times-Herald* Invitation, I pause from competition long enough to say hello to my former college roommate and vaulting partner, Frank Estes. (Photo by Ron Scribner.)

When you're preparing to attempt 19 feet, it isn't much different from contemplating jumping out of a third-story window.

Above, top: Seven years ago Earl Bell (right) was a world-record holder in the pole vault and one of the athletes I greatly admired. Today we're the friendliest of adversaries, both bidding for spots on the U.S. Olympic team. E. B. is one of the finest athletes and best people I've ever known. Above, bottom: My dad liked the idea of my showing up at meets in a T-shirt that advertised his SOS Bail Bond company. The beard, which I wore briefly during the 1984 indoor season, was a different matter. (Photos by Ron Scribner.)

If your run is good and you plant the pole properly, the next step is a free ride toward the bar. (Photos this page and opposite page, top, by Ron Scribner. Photo opposite page, bottom, by Victor G. Sailor, courtesy *Track & Field News*.)

(Photo by Ron Scribner.)

5

Coming of Age

THE ATHLETIC ODYSSEY of Frank Estes had come to another fork in the road, and the talented young Abilene pole vaulter was concerned that the next turn might lead to a dead end. He had been a standout performer for Abilene Cooper at the time Billy Olson was just beginning to consider giving up golf, then had gone to the University of Texas where, as a sophomore, he had won the Southwest Conference championship.

But for a variety of reasons things had turned sour at UT. After long consideration, he had chosen to transfer to Northeast Louisiana State, a small university in Monroe, Louisiana which has a national reputation as a track-and-field power.

Still discontent, Estes had not found what he was looking for there, either.

Returning to Abilene for the Easter holidays in the spring of 1977, he learned that Billy Olson, a vaulter two years his junior, had transferred from Baylor to Abilene Christian.

"I remember going out to ACU and vaulting in a meet they were having while I was home," Estes says, "and the minute I saw how well Billy was vaulting I knew where I was supposed to be. If I was going to reach the potential I felt I had as a pole vaulter, I needed to be around someone who had goals similar to mine—someone really dedicated to what he was doing.

"Billy and I talked and I told him of my concerns. He suggested I transfer to ACU. 'Come on back home where you belong,' he said. 'We can get an apartment and room together and vault and put everything in the past behind us.'

83

"He'd gone through the transfer business himself and knew it wasn't an easy thing to do. But he gave me one of those 'life's-too-short' lectures and encouraged me to get myself into an environment where I would be happy and able to concentrate on vaulting.

"From that moment on we were best of friends. What he was proposing was a very unselfish thing. He was, in effect, saying, 'Come on, I'll help you and you help me and maybe we both can be good at this.'

"That's one of the unique things about track and field. Most athletes I've ever known in other sports jealously guard their own status as king of the hill. If you're the top man at your school, the last thing you want is someone to come in who might endanger your position. But track's not that way. Neither Billy nor I knew at that point which of us was going to be the better vaulter. But we both knew we could improve with the other's help.

"In all probability, I probably would never have considered going back to Abilene and ACU if Billy hadn't encouraged me to do so. But that move, and all the things that would happen afterwards, provided the turning point of my life. I owe Billy a lot for that. A lot."

If I've ever had a hero, someone I looked up to and wanted to be like, it was Frank Estes. When I was first getting interested in vaulting, he was something of a local celebrity, and I spent a great deal of time wondering if I'd ever be as good as he was.

Even after he'd come to Abilene Christian and we shared an apartment, I held him in awe. In fact, I emulated him—mannerisms, gestures—to a point where I'm sure it bothered him at times. And it wasn't just that he was a good pole vaulter. It was his honesty, his sincerity. In very short order he showed me what a true friend is supposed to be—someone you can trust completely. He taught me a lot of valuable lessons that have absolutely nothing to do with athletics.

To pay for the apartment we were living in, we both got jobs waiting on tables at local restaurants. And when we weren't working or in class or at the practice field, we sat around, talking.

As it turned out, we were alike in a number of ways. In high school and his early college years, Frank had been quite a party-goer, never too serious about much of anything. Some of his stories had a very familiar ring to me. But by the time he came back to Abilene he had really settled down, was a pretty serious sort, and had taken a strong interest in the Baptist church.

And to this day I've never known an athlete who worked harder at being the very best he could be. Frank is only about 5 foot 8— short for a vaulter, but he worked at his technique, constantly perfecting it.

He was also an outstanding competitor. In fact, it was Frank Estes who taught me what a real competitive drive is all about. Of all the things he's done for me, I'd have to say that's probably the most valuable gift—aside from his friendship—he's given me. He impressed on me the fact that if one has a gift for something he is obligated to work at it and make the best of it.

In the evenings we would set up two projectors and watch films of the top vaulters in the world, following their vaults frame by frame, looking for things we might be able to use to better our own performances. I would watch vaulters like Bob Seagren, Dave Roberts, and Earl Bell because they were all about the same size I was. Frank, on the other hand, studied the style and technique of a Swedish vaulter named Kjell Isaksson who had set the world record in 1970.

There were few times when pole vaulting was ever very far from our thoughts. We lived it, breathed it, and constantly talked of goals we hoped to attain. It was great having someone around who understood what all the work and practice and dreaming was all about.

Under the rules of the NAIA (National Association of Intercollegiate Athletics), Frank would be eligible to compete for ACU in December, and the timing couldn't have been better. For both of us it would be our first chance to participate in the national collegiate indoor championship meet.

I don't suppose we could have started things off on a better note. At the national championships we each cleared 16 feet, 6 inches and tied for first place. We were on our way.

And, to add to the thrill of it all, Abilene Christian tied with Jackson State for the team championship.

As the outdoor season got underway, it looked as if ACU was

going to dominate the pole vault everywhere we went. The first major outdoor meet of the year was the Border Olympics in Laredo, Texas, and I managed to win with a jump of 16 feet, 9 inches. Frank was second, and a couple of other vaulters on our team, Don Lee and Ronnie Hunt, were third and fourth.

That's the way it went for much of the season. We all seemed to carry each other along. We were all progressing because of each other. I dare say none of us would have been doing as well as we were had we been at different schools rather than working together. It was as if we had our own little fraternity.

I was delighted by the fact that I was improving steadily and was also pleased to see that Frank was returning to the form he'd shown while at the University of Texas. Early in the season, he cleared 17 feet, 6 inches in a meet in Baton Rouge (I was second, a foot behind him), and then returned to Austin to win the Texas Relays (while I gloriously no-heighted).

Frank cleared 17-6 in Mexico City and had an excellent attempt at 18 feet. It looked as if he was ready to make a big breakthrough. He even made the finals of the 200-meter dash and finished a strong second in the race. On a lark, I had tried the event, too, and finished third in his preliminary heat, not making the finals but feeling good in the knowledge that my speed, something vitally essential to pole-vaulting success, was improving.

Both of us, in fact, were feeling good about our progress, confident that it was going to be an exceptional year.

Then misfortune struck. The week after we returned from Mexico City, Frank badly pulled a hamstring muscle. He was in such pain that all the color drained from his face. Coach Hood examined the injury and immediately instructed the trainers to carry Frank to his pickup.

I rode with them to the office of Frank's dad, an Abilene doctor, holding an ice pack on the injured leg, which was already badly discolored. Frank was silent during the trip, a picture of dejection, and there was nothing I could say to lift his spirits. He knew the injury was serious and that it would, in all likelihood, keep him away from pole vaulting for quite some time.

After examining the damage, his father made it official: Frank's season was over.

It's strange how things can change so quickly, can go from rose colored to pitch black in the flick of an eye at the least-expected moment. My friend's injury drained him of confidence and enthusiasm for life, just as if someone had pulled a plug.

For weeks he was despondent, staying around the apartment and away from the track. It was as if he was on automatic pilot, going to class by rote motion, eating only when I suggested we go to the cafeteria. It was a difficult time for him, and I'm afraid I was little help. I tried to encourage him, telling him that he would be back, better than ever. But, in retrospect, I suspect my chatter had something of an insincere ring to it. I was no more sure he would be vaulting again than he was.

I prayed he would be okay and that he would regain the magnificent spirit I'd seen in him before the injury. Then I went back to work at my own business.

There were goals I had set for myself, and it seemed foolish to let Frank's absence affect what I felt I had to do. I wanted to win the NAIA outdoor championship, I wanted to get to a point where I was consistently vaulting over 17 feet, and I wanted to break the national age-group record, which UCLA's Mike Tully held. If I could clear 17-10½ before I turned 20, I could hold the national junior record.

As the spring went on, I progressed steadily. I was vaulting over 17 feet regularly, as I had hoped to be; I won the NAIA title; and I surprised even myself in my first encounter with what I considered the best pole vaulters in the United States.

Coach Hood stopped me one afternoon as I was walking toward the track and told me he felt it was time to see how I might fare against the top vaulters in the country. At the TAC (The Athletics Congress) national meet in Los Angeles, he said, every standout collegiate jumper, as well as most of those competing for club teams, would be on hand.

He told me he had already entered me in the competition.

I must admit that, while I was steadily improving, I honestly didn't feel I was near the level of the Earl Bells and Mike Tullys of the world. I was getting closer, maybe, but never in my wildest imagination did I think I was ready seriously to challenge them. Still, the idea of competing with them at the TAC meet was exciting. If nothing else, just being exposed to that level of competition would benefit me. I still had a lot to learn, and the vaulters I would be facing in Los Angeles were the finest teachers I knew of.

The meet was held on the campus of UCLA and was, as all U.S. national championships are, a gathering of track-and-field all-stars: Olympians, world and American record holders, NCAA champions, and veteran performers who were on hand to defend titles they had been winning for several years.

When I managed to make the finals of the pole vault, clearing 17 feet, 2¾ inches, I was feeling pretty good about myself.

That changed quickly, thanks in part to Coach Hood's fondness for Chinese food. The night before the finals he took me to a restaurant which he insisted was one of the best in Southern California. But for one who has always felt a balanced meal was a double cheeseburger in each hand, the menu wasn't exactly a dream come true. I ate sweet-and-sour this and chop-suey that as my dinner companion extolled the virtues of the Chinese dietary habits.

I'm not sure what the message was in the fortune cookie I was served after dinner, but I do know it gave no hint that I would spend most of the night in the motel bathroom, throwing up and thinking how nice it would feel to just die and get it all over with.

The next day in the finals I was unable even to clear the opening height.

I returned to Abilene with two resolves: I would never again be lured into a Chinese restaurant, and I was going to return to the national meet again the following year and prove to all on hand that my failure in the finals was not a matter of folding under the pressure of the competition.

In the meantime, there was the national age-group record to think about. With my twentieth birthday fast approaching, time was running out. If I was going to break Mike Tully's record, I'd have to get in high gear.

Since the record books clearly state that a new mark can only be accepted if it is attained during a regulation track meet, with a full complement of competitors, Coach Hood set about planning a series of "all-comers" meets to be staged at the ACU track. The events would be open to anyone who wished to compete—high-school athletes from the local schools and those in the Abilene area, collegians who were looking for summer competition, whomever.

My competition in the pole vault was made up of teammates who had decided to remain in Abilene for the summer and several high-school vaulters, including a promising all-round athlete, named Brad Pursley, from the neighboring community of Merkel.

The first of the three meets Coach Hood had arranged was run a month before my birthday. It was no secret in Abilene that the meet was being held for my benefit and that I was trying to break the age-group record.

The afternoon of the meet all three local television stations were on hand, as were photographers from the paper. Everyone stood around the pole-vault pit, ignoring the rest of the meet that was going on, ready to record my history-making jump.

It never came. In better shape than I'd ever been, I felt confident when I cleared 17 feet, 5 inches with ease. But despite three relatively good jumps at 17-10½, I didn't make it. The TV cameras were packed up, the stands quickly emptied, and everyone went home. Maybe next time, I said weakly. I felt like a stage magician whose big trick hadn't worked.

But everyone was back a couple of weeks later for the second try, cameras ready, notebooks poised. I cleared 17-6 and then had the bar moved up to the record height again. I should have cleared it on all three attempts. I was well over the bar each time, but hit it coming down. Once it was my chest, another time I didn't get my arm back far enough as I began my fall and touched the bar with my forearm.

Tully's record was beginning to look safe.

The third and final try was scheduled for the second week in July, just a week before my birthday. Most of the familiar faces were there—athletes who had come to try to improve their 100-yard dash times or run in a couple of relays or see if they might be cut out to be a high jumper. This time, however, the media evidently found something more interesting to do.

In view of the fact they'd gone back empty-handed on two previous trips, I couldn't blame them.

As the competition got underway, I was initially glad they

weren't there. Feeling lifeless, I barely made 17 feet. The next logical progression would have been to go up to 17-4 or 17-6, but since I was the only one left in the competition I decided to go for broke. In truth, I had decided to speed things up and get it over with. I had the bar moved up to 17-10¾. I was beginning to sound like a broken record.

Coach Hood came over to wish me well and asked how I felt. "Great," I lied.

Then, with a vault that was far from being a technical masterpiece, I cleared the height with room to spare. The record I had been chasing most of the season had finally come at the most unexpected time. All of which proves beyond a doubt that you can never anticipate what might happen in this business of pole vaulting.

Later that afternoon, as I stood in the shower in the dressing room, savoring the warm spray and the knowledge that I had finally achieved a goal I regarded as important, I found myself in a reflective mood. It was as if the breaking of the record had brought a sweeping calm over me. The pressures of the season, most of them self-imposed, were gone, and it felt good to relax, to let the water pour over my body and the silence keep me company.

If anyone had happened upon me at that moment and asked if I was at peace with the world, I would have given them an instant yes. The decision to transfer from Baylor to Abilene Christian, to retreat to the comfortable surrounds of home, had proved to be a good one; I had good friends whom I respected and who respected me; and I was making progress as an athlete. What else would a person want?

It would be some time before I could come up with an honest answer to that question. There *was* something missing in my life, but at the time I wasn't bothering to look around and find out what it was.

Coach Don Hood knew. But he took carefully measured steps toward pointing out the fact that there was more to life than good times and gold medals and breaking records.

"One of the first things some coaches tell kids they're trying to

recruit, kids who have expressed an interest in our school, is that they'll be required to go to church regularly if they choose to enroll at Abilene Christian.

"I've always looked on that as a positive statement. If another coach thinks he's hurting our chances by pointing that out to a youngster, then I think he's mistaken.

"Sure, we have regular chapel services which students are required to attend. We make no apologies for that, or for the fact that we have strong feelings about clean living and a Christian attitude. But we don't brainwash people who come to us.

"Though Billy was the product of a Christian home, he had very few positive feelings about religion when he came to ACU. He was forever looking for an excuse to get out of going to chapel services, and when we would stop en route home from track meets to attend Sunday church services, he was the first to complain.

"There was one time, I remember, when he asked if we couldn't just get on home. I made an announcement to everyone that it would be perfectly okay for anyone who didn't want to go to church to stay in the van while the rest of us attended services. At first, Billy just sat there while everyone else walked toward the church.

"I wanted to go back and try to persuade him to join us, but didn't. My philosophy has always been that you can't push people in such matters. So I just went on into the church with the rest of the team. A couple of minutes later, Billy came quietly walking down the aisle and joined us.

"It wasn't that he was rebellious about religion. He simply saw no reason to actively participate, to learn, to develop a closer relationship with God."

At the time, it was a state of affairs that concerned Don Hood far more than it did Billy Olson.

"See, I had strong feelings that Billy was going to develop into an exceptional athlete. The things he had accomplished in the early stages of his career were nothing compared to what I felt reasonably sure he was going to do.

"And I knew that as his stature as an athlete grew he was going to be in a very influential position. On trips I talked with him about it some, never making a big issue of it. But I wanted him to think about the fact that he was going to develop into the kind of person a lot of

younger kids would be looking up to. And there would be older people looking for faults.

"I just tried to make him aware of the fact he was going to be in a position of influence—and that he had to decide whether he wanted that influence to be positive or negative. I didn't press the issue, but I did want him to begin thinking about things like that."

It wasn't that I didn't consider myself a Christian. After all, I had grown up in a Christian home and had been raised in the Baptist church. But I had never been able fully to commit myself to things like Bible study and faithful attendance to Sunday services and chapel. In truth, I really didn't understand what it was all about and didn't want to dedicate the time and effort to find out.

My sins, I felt, were relatively minor, and I did know right from wrong. That, it seemed to me, was enough. If others felt a strong need for religion in their lives, that was fine with me. To each his own. But I failed to see the enjoyment.

For me, pole vaulting and good times were all I needed. At least that's what I thought as I reached my twentieth birthday.

I simply couldn't see how attending chapel daily was going to help me eventually clear 18 feet in the pole vault.

When I returned to school for my second year of eligibility, Coach Hood outlined an ambitious indoor-season schedule for me. I had enjoyed the few indoor meets in which I had participated, and I had done reasonably well in them, so the news that I would be competing on a regular basis during the fall was exciting.

Too, the schedule Coach Hood had planned would again afford me more chances to vault against the best. If I was to make a name for myself, it would have to be against Tully of UCLA and Bell of Arkansas State, the two top-rated collegiate pole vaulters in the country.

Adding to the excitement I was feeling for the new season at hand was the fact that Frank Estes, once again healthy and in high spirits, would rejoin workouts. For that matter, we would have enough vaulters working every afternoon to conduct our own track meets. In addition to Frank and me, there were Don Lee, a 17-¾ vaulter who had decided to follow Frank's footsteps and transfer from the University of Texas, and Ron Hunt, a transfer from a California junior college who had a personal best of 16-2.

Then there was also Brad Pursley, the freshman from Merkel High School who I felt was going to develop quickly into one of the best around. Because of the tremendous depth we had, however, Coach Hood decided to redshirt Brad his freshman year so that he might still have four years of eligibility remaining after some of our other vaulters had graduated.

All in all, we had a great workout situation. Everyone was eager to improve his own abilities, but equally ready to lend a hand to his teammates.

We were already talking about the possibility of placing 1-2-3-4 at the NAIA championships.

Describing an indoor track meet is difficult. About the closest comparison I can make is with a three-ring circus. In a confined area—generally an area where hockey or basketball is usually played—a banked board track, 160–200 yards to a lap, is installed. And while runners are busy elbowing each other for position on this small running surface, the field events are going on in the infield area. At any given time, a pole vaulter might be preparing to jump, a high jumper getting ready at another corner of the arena, and the shot putters warming up on the other end of the building. It's constant action with the crowds right on top of you.

And I must admit I love it. The noise, the excitement, the fast pace, and the interaction with the people in the stands really gets my competitive juices flowing.

So it was that a whole new world opened to me that winter of 1978. I learned about the headaches of having your poles traveling to one destination while you were flying to another, about the need to dress for blizzard conditions when traveling to meets in the East. And I learned that the fraternity of world-class pole vaulters was one not just anyone was allowed entrance to.

Those already initiated made it clear that a newcomer from Abilene, Texas, had to prove himself before the welcome mat was spread.

It was in January that I competed in the Catholic Youth Organization Indoor Games in College Park, Maryland, clearing 17 feet to finish third to Tully and Bell. Then, at the East Coast Invitational in Richmond, Virginia, I won with a jump of 16-6.

By February I had been invited to participate in the Millrose Games in Madison Square Garden. The meet, one of the most storied on the indoor circuit, annually draws a who's who of track and field—and I wasn't quite there yet. Dan Ripley gave the crowd its money's worth, clearing 18 feet, 1½ inches. Despite the fact that I set a new school record, clearing 17-4½, I could do no better than fifth in the field.

I was back in New York for the Vitalis-Olympic Invitational and found even more competition. Gunther Lohre, an outstanding vaulter from East Germany, was there and won, beating Tully for the gold medal. I managed third place, despite the fact that I jumped only 16 feet, 8¾ inches.

At the Philadelphia Track Classic, I enjoyed one of the high-lights of my career. By clearing 17 feet, I managed to score an upset victory over Tully, the number-one-ranked college vaulter in the U.S.

Then, at the NAIA indoor championships in Kansas City, the Abilene Christian pole-vault brotherhood very nearly succeeded in accomplishing its goal—we finished 1-2-3. I won with a jump of 17-6½, Don Lee was second, and Frank Estes, rounding back into shape, was third.

While the winter season had been one in which there were more defeats than victories, the experience had been invaluable to me. I was beginning to feel I could vault with the best.

I was also getting the distinct impression that I wasn't any threat to win Most Popular Pole Vaulter if the voting was done by other vaulters.

"We're all guilty of making snap judgments about people," says three-time NCAA pole-vault champion Earl Bell, "but the truth of the matter is that there was just something about Billy that rubbed me the wrong way when I first met him.

"Terry Porter, another pole vaulter, had been telling me that he was one of those up-and-coming vaulters we had all better keep an eye on. When I first saw him, with his long hair and skinny legs, I

*immediately made up my mind that he wasn't going to be anybody's
great worry.*

*"But—and, remember, this is before he was really jumping
high—he carried himself in such a manner that suggested he was
there to take over. About the most diplomatic thing I can say is that I
simply didn't like the guy. I think we had a values conflict.*

*"For quite some time we didn't get along. But he was just a kid
then. As he matured he began to realize that he wasn't the center of
the universe. And as he realized that he also became a much better
pole vaulter.*

*"Today, Billy and I are good friends. I have great admiration for
him not only as an athlete, but also as a person. It's been fun watching him grow over the years. The better he's gotten as a vaulter, the
less impressed he's become with himself. And that, to me, is the
mark of a real champion."*

Looking back, I hate to think that if one had looked up "self-
centered" in the dictionary it might have said, ". . . see Billy
Olson." But I'm afraid Earl had me pegged.

On the other hand, I like to think that maybe the awe I felt in the
presence of vaulters I had long judged to be the best around had
something to do with the perception he and others had of me.
Frankly, I was a little self-conscious around them, and I might
have tried to cover that with an outward display of confidence. All I
know is that I had tremendous respect for them and wanted badly
for them to feel the same toward me. The camaraderie I saw among
them, among guys who were battling each other to be the best in
the world, impressed me greatly.

But I wasn't a part of it. And I wasn't sure how to be. It was
another area in which I still had a lot to learn.

As the collegiate outdoor season came to an end, Frank and I
were ranked second and third behind UCLA's Mike Tully among
college vaulters. I had cleared 17 feet, 6¾ inches to win the NAIA
outdoor title (upping my winning streak to four in a row), and
Frank had finished second.

I had lost some during the year, but I had finally begun to de-

velop the kind of consistency I felt necessary to become an outstanding vaulter. Even back when I was in high school, I had never
been very impressed with a guy who managed to record one really
outstanding jump but who could not come close to equaling it in the
weeks afterwards. The good ones, to my way of thinking, are those
who manage to clear impressive heights week after week. That
was what I was shooting for.

It has always been my philosophy that if one gets to a point
where he can clear a certain height with regularity, his chances of
going considerably higher on one of those days when everything
seems to fall into place are greatly increased. That, I think, is how
world records are set. Regardless of the event, you're generally
going to find that the athlete who sets a world record has been
performing at very near that level for quite some time.

At the TAAF (The Amateur Athletics Federation) Championships in Wichita, Tully and I got into a pretty exciting dual, which
ended with his beating me on fewer misses as we both cleared 17
feet, 10½ inches. And Frank wasn't far back at 17-6.

Frank's and my efforts and those of an ACU quarter-miler
named Randy Baker caught the eye of a West Coast sports enthusi-
ast named Dr. Paul Burns. He was the driving force of the Maccabi
Track Club and asked if we would be interested in coming to California and competing for his club in a few meets during the
summer.

I need not tell you how long it took us to make our decision,
particularly after he suggested that we headquarter at his Malibu
beach house during our stay.

It sounded light years better than water skiing at Possum Kingdom Lake in Texas, so we agreed to be in California just as soon as
classes were dismissed for the semester. We left in Randy Baker's
car the day after classes ended.

It was the kind of summer vacation you read about in books or
see in the movies. Dr. Burns's home was right on the beach. Each
morning we would run on the sand, then swim for a while. Each
afternoon we would travel to a nearby practice field in a Mercedes-
Benz. If we decided to go into Los Angeles for a movie, Dr. Burns's
Jaguar was available.

All that, plus the fact that he had persuaded promoters of four meets to include us in their field. The first was a meet in Eugene, Oregon. First-class airline tickets, the works.

When he took us in to Los Angeles International, however, problems developed. Our poles, we were told, would not fit on the plane we were scheduled to be on. Dr. Burns hurried around, found us another flight that would get us to Portland, and gave us money for a rental car. We were cutting it thin, he said, but he would call the meet director and tell him we were coming and might be a little late.

He didn't know anything about the lead-foot driving abilities of Yours Truly. We landed in Portland, picked out a shiny, new Trans-Am, tied our poles on top, and set sail. We arrived just as the competitors in the pole vault were being called.

Despite little time to warm up, I had a good day, making every height I attempted on my first try. Tully won at 18 feet, and I was second at 17-6. But I felt good and should have gone higher.

Later, as we were driving back to Portland at a more leisurely—and legal—rate of speed, Frank said, "Okay, you've been flirting with 18 feet for over a month now. I thought you would get it today, in fact. But it's going to come soon, real soon. You're ready. You just need to make your mind up that you're going to do it."

I thought about it all the way back to Los Angeles. Maybe it *was* time. I hoped so.

The following afternoon wasn't it, however. Dr. Burns drove us over to a meet being held at Compton Junior College. Obviously the meet directors hadn't spent a great deal of time or money on the pole-vault facility. The pit, such as it was, was much smaller than the regulation 16-by-16-foot landing area you find at collegiate competitions.

Frank looked at it and suggested we turn around and head back to the beach. "If we get up very high," he said, "it's going to look like we're falling onto a postage stamp."

As it turned out, Frank and I were the only vaulters on hand. We were actually to give an exhibition rather than compete. The public-address announcer made a big production about "two of the greatest college pole vaulters in America" being on hand. Even the legendary Wilt Chamberlain came by to say hello and tell us how much he was looking forward to seeing us jump.

So we did. We both cleared 16-6 and then chickened out when the officials running the event suggested we try harder. We politely explained about the hard trip we'd made the day before, thanked them kindly, and headed back to the beach. Dr. Burns, we decided, had done us no favors with that meet.

But there were a couple of more attractive ones coming up. And, there was a scheduled visit to an executive with a company that makes running shoes. Randy, Frank, and I had been told by Dr. Burns that this man would like for us to drop by his house for a visit. He had suggested he might have a couple of pair of new shoes he would like for us to try out.

The trip proved to be a bonanza. After sitting in his living room, talking about the recent meets we'd been to, he asked us to follow him into the garage. Inside, the place looked like a shoe store. Boxes of shoes lined each wall, stacked all the way to the ceiling.

"Help yourselves," he said. It was like turning three kids loose in a candy store.

You should understand that there is tremendous competition among the makers of athletic shoes. In the professional sports ranks, in fact, it is not at all uncommon for an athlete to sign a multimillion-dollar contract with a particular manufacturer, promising only to wear its shoes exclusively.

But for three modestly successful athletes from Abilene, Texas, free shoes were quite enough. We left with the trunk of the car filled. "I'll tell you what," Randy said as we drove back to Dr. Burns's, "the meets and the beach and all have been nice, but I'd have made the trip out here just for these shoes."

Fighting the traffic on the L.A. Freeway, we laughed and sang and swore eternal loyalty to the makers of those track shoes.

The following weekend, I was wearing a brand-new pair of spikes and thinking about what Frank had said to me about 18 feet, when I pulled a groin muscle early in the competition. I didn't even clear the opening height.

In pain and frustrated by the sudden turn of events, I sat by and watched Mike Tully win with a vault of 17 feet, 6 inches. Frank, who was vaulting as well as I've ever seen him, was second.

Following the meet, Dr. Burns had trainers check my injury, talked with them at length, then told me it looked as if my season was over. With but one week remaining before the TAC national championships, I couldn't even jog, much less run.

So, while everyone else worked out every afternoon at UCLA, I went to the movies.

I've always been able to come back from injuries quickly, however, and toward the end of the week the pain had disappeared. Though not nearly as confident as I pretended to be, I told Dr. Burns that I felt I could jump. He wasn't crazy about the idea, fearful that I might do even further damage to the injury, and only agreed after I promised him that if the leg gave me any trouble at any stage during the competition I would withdraw.

Thus I traveled with Frank to Mt. San Antonio College, hoping the leg would hold up and that there would be no Chinese food restaurants within miles of the place. I badly wanted to do better than I had the previous year.

As we made our way out to the stadium, I put the injury out of my mind and thought of how there had been six different occasions during the seasons when I'd been close to clearing 18 feet. Every time, though, there had been some minor technical flaw that had caused me to miss. The pursuit was becoming frustrating, but I felt mentally ready.

It was the physical part I wasn't too sure of. I made it through the preliminaries and into the finals with only minor discomfort in the leg.

In the finals I cleared 17-3 on my second attempt. Then, I made 17 feet, 8 inches on my second try at that height. The leg was beginning to really hurt, but the adrenaline was really pumping. I felt I could make it through at least a couple more jumps.

When the bar was raised to 18 feet, ½ inch, there were five vaulters still in the competition. Tully cleared it on his first try.

As the official called my name, I walked to the top of the runway, thinking about all the other times I had tried the height, of how close I had come, and of how wearisome the burden of not making it over the 18-foot barrier had grown.

I went about everything meticulously, making sure my marks were right on the runway, that my grip on the pole was just right. When you are trying for that kind of height, Coach Hood had repeatedly told me, you have to challenge it. Go at it full speed; don't hold anything back. I reminded myself of his lectures. The time, just as Frank had said, had come.

Even before I planted the pole in the box I had a good feeling. Everything seemed right. I rode the pole for as long as possible, then made my turn over the bar, arched my back and threw my body backwards.

I knew I had cleared it even before I landed in the pit. Finally, I was an 18-foot vaulter. It was as if a mountain of weight had been lifted from my shoulders.

Never have I felt such a mixture of feelings; relief, happiness, and pain all ran together. I didn't know whether to laugh or cry.

Even before I could climb out of the pit, Frank was there, hugging me, shaking my hand, celebrating with me. "I told you, didn't I?" he kept yelling.

Indeed, he had. And I hoped he realized how big a part he had played in my accomplishment.

That Tully went on to win the competition did nothing to dampen my spirits. Second place in the TAC national championships sounded just fine to me. It was, in fact, a little like waking up on Christmas morning. Not only had I cleared 18 feet and done it in a major meet against the best competition in the United States, but my second-place finish earned me a spot on the American team that would participate in the Pan-American Games in San Juan, Puerto Rico and the World Student Games in Mexico City.

The season, which just a few days earlier I had feared might be over, was going to stretch deeper into the summer.

To do well in those international meets, however, I knew I had to get the injury behind me. The day after the TAC meet I was so sore I could hardly walk. It was time to go home. A couple of weeks' rest, I decided, would resolve the problem; then I could get back to training for the meets ahead.

Patience, however, is not one of my virtues. After staying away from the vaulting pit for ten days, I was considering testing the leg when Dr. Burns called to say that Frank and I had been invited to compete in the Meet of Champions in Philadelphia.

I explained to Dr. Burns that I wasn't sure the leg was ready and that I was hesitant to risk reinjuring it with the Pan-Am Games

just around the corner. "They want you up there," he said. "Just go
and make an appearance. If you can jump, fine; if not, that's okay,
too." I wasn't too hot on the idea of going and just standing around,
so I made up my mind to try to vault. And I knew that Frank,
disappointed by his eighth place finish at the national meet, was
anxious to compete in Philadelphia.

Once there, I realized I had made a big mistake. When I tried to
warm up, I couldn't get out of a trot. So I went in search of the meet
director to let him know that I wouldn't be jumping. When I told
him so, he blew his stack. Obviously, he had not been made aware
of my injury and had not planned for me to fly up and "make an
appearance." I spent the rest of the day making sure I was well
removed from his path.

While it was a less-than-memorable day for me, Frank was at
his best. With Tully and Earl Bell in the field, he cleared a personal
best of 17-6¾ and won the event.

I've never seen him happier, and I knew how he felt. He had won
against the best in the nation in his last major meet of the season
and was already talking about his goals for the following year as
we headed back to Abilene.

By the time I left for San Juan I was feeling terrible. My leg was
still hurting me. I had also missed quite a bit of training time and
was concerned that my technique might be a bit rusty. I was far
from confident.

The fact that Tully had decided not to make the trip, giving up
his spot to Greg Woepse, third-place finisher at the TAC meet,
enhanced my chances of winning.

The Pan-American Games are something of a Western hemi-
sphere Olympics, held every four years. In addition to track and
field, there is a full complement of other international competition: swimming, baseball, boxing, cycling, judo, basketball, and
more. I found the atmosphere exciting and enjoyed meeting athletes from so many other countries. Also, it was a thrill to be
wearing for the first time a uniform with U.S.A. across the chest.

As the days passed and time for the pole-vault competition
neared, I found myself getting more and more eager to compete.

Then, however, hurdler Renaldo Nehemiah arrived. Late getting to San Juan, he showed up with a galloping case of the flu. A day later I had it. I couldn't even get out of bed. The team doctor came by periodically to see if I was making any headway toward recovery (which I wasn't) and finally told me he had informed the coach I would be unable to compete.

To this day I'm convinced I might have died there in a foreign country had it not been for Louise Ritter, a fellow Texan who had made the team as a high jumper. Every few hours she would check by my room, bringing me soft drinks, forcing me to take medication, and generally playing nurse.

On the day of the pole-vault finals I was well enough to sit in the stands and watch Woepse, my roommate who had somehow managed to avoid catching Renaldo's bug, win the silver medal.

I decided that sitting in the crowd, watching others compete, was not something I wanted to do on a regular basis. It was a strange— and disappointing—feeling to be there, representing the United States, but unable to do anything but cheer others on.

On the international scene, Billy Olson wasn't exactly setting the woods on fire.

A shoe company representative I had met in Puerto Rico offered me a chance to redeem myself, however. His company was sending a delegation of athletes to Europe for a series of meets in Sweden, Denmark, Switzerland, and Italy, and he invited me to be a part of the team.

It was a wonderful experience, traveling through foreign countries and seeing the lifestyle of people who had previously existed only in textbooks for me. Adding to my enjoyment of it all was the fact the pain had gone from my leg and I performed reasonably well in each meet. I was generally jumping in the 16-8 and 16-10 range.

But by the time the two-week tour came to an end I was anxious to get home, to put my vaulting pole away for a while, and rest. But I still had to compete in the World Student Games in Mexico City. I cleared only 17 feet, 2¾ inches, finishing eight in an Olympic-caliber field that included the top valuters from Russia, France, and Poland.

I was hardly prepared for the news I would receive upon my arrival back in Abilene.

While his teammate was touring Europe, Frank Estes was in Abilene taking it easy. The success he had enjoyed in Philadelphia had ended his season on a high note, he felt, and he was satisfied to take a few months off from vaulting before turning his attention to the next season.

However, when Coach Hood approached him with the news that he was taking a few athletes to a TAAF state meet in Waco and asked if he would like to go along, Frank went in search of the poles he had stored away.

"I was still in good shape," Estes remembers, "and it sounded like fun. I knew there wouldn't be a great deal of competition there, so it would be more like a good workout than anything else. And, in the back of my mind I was thinking that it might be nice to take a crack at the meet record.

"It was one of those ideal central-Texas summer nights with no wind at all. I began vaulting when the bar got to 16 feet and made it easily. Then I cleared 16-6 and won the competition. Feeling strong, I had the bar raised to 16-9, an inch above the record, and cleared that on my first jump.

"After talking with the meet officials, I decided to see if I could raise the record a little more. I had the bar moved to 17 feet."

On his first jump, Estes realized he wasn't going to make it and, in the vernacular of the event, "bailed out." Rather than try to complete the jump, he released the pole and let himself fall.

The angle of his fall, however, was off-course, and he missed the pit completely, landing on concrete. He hit on his knees and hands and tried to break his fall, but to little avail. His head smashed into the concrete and he was knocked unconscious.

At the hospital, doctors advised a concerned Don Hood that his young vaulter had fractured his skull in three places.

Today, five years after that harrowing night in Waco, Texas, Frank Estes admits that the accident had a great deal to do with his decision to quit the sport he had so long devoted his life to.

When I got home from Europe, Frank still had two black eyes

and was bothered with headaches. But it wasn't the physical problems that I noticed first. There was a look in his eye, a kind of brooding resignation that disturbed me.

Even before he mentioned it, I feared that he was thinking about giving up vaulting, and I simply could not understand it. It had to be more than the accident. Frank was too courageous for that to be the only reason.

But his enthusiasm, the enthusiasm I had seen just weeks earlier when he won in Philadelphia, was gone, as if it had been drained from him while in the hospital in Waco.

When he did finally begin to talk of quitting, I argued with him. He had obviously made up his mind and was comfortable with his decision. But, rather than accept it as I should have, I stayed after him to give it one more try. I badgered and begged. I reminded him that an Olympic year was just around the corner, that we had talked of making the team together.

Finally, he agreed that maybe he would think it over. I felt I had won a major victory. It just didn't seem right for the pole vaulter I admired above all others, the athlete I considered the finest competitor I'd ever known, to suddenly call it quits at the height of his career.

In retrospect, I pressured too much. Frank's trips to the weight room and out to the vaulting pit were more for my benefit than his. The spark was gone. What had once been enjoyable and meaningful to him had turned into drudgery. Frank had been vaulting for ten years, since the seventh grade, and it had become tedious to him. The accident in Waco, certainly, was part of the problem. But it was compounded by the fact he had grown weary of the 35 to 40 hours of workouts every week.

His eligibility at ACU had run out, and there was no longer a scholarship to depend on, no more team to compete for.

It was in October that Coach Hood invited us to accompany him on a trip to Taiwan where he was to conduct a coaching clinic. Frank and I were to vault in a meet which was to be held in conjunction with Hood's lectures.

The return to competition, I hoped, would rekindle Frank's enthusiasm. But no luck. I cleared 17 feet, 8½ inches. Frank didn't make the opening height.

It was his last meet.

Looking back, I can better understand his decision. There are times now when the workouts and the travel wear on me far more than they once did. The time, I suppose, will come when I'll feel the same way he did.

But I miss having him around in the weight room late at night when I don't want to do the work I know I need to be doing. I miss vaulting with him and traveling with him.

Frank's living in Odessa now, happily married and doing quite well in the restaurant business. He's promised me he'll never have Chinese food on his menu.

6

New Highs, New Lows

THE SPRING SEMESTER of 1980 had been underway for almost two weeks before I set foot in a classroom. Invitations to compete in indoor meets had picked up considerably in the wake of my improvement during the previous outdoor season, and I wasn't turning any of them down. The experience, I felt, would be invaluable.

My tardy enrollment was the result of a trip to Paris for a meet, then a further delay while I flew directly from France to Canada for the *Toronto Star*-Maple Leaf Games. It wouldn't show up on my transcript, but I was getting a pretty good lesson in geography.

Frankly, since I was hardly a legitimate candidate to make the Dean's List, I can't say I worried a great deal about my late academic start. I was vaulting well, was again healthy, so everything seemed in order. School was the "necessary evil" part of my life.

Still, it was good to get back home and return to familiar surroundings where I understood the language and didn't have to live out of a suitcase.

At the risk of dwelling on my still lukewarm attitude toward higher education, I suppose I should admit that I wasn't exactly taking the kind of class load with which the great scholars earn reputations. It had become my practice to avoid too many demanding courses in the spring so that I could concentrate as much as possible on vaulting. After all, 1980 was to be a special year, with the Olympic Games scheduled to be held in Moscow. I was beginning to think maybe I had a chance at making the United States team.

One of the first classes I did manage to finally get to upon my return was—are you ready for this?—"Introductory Bowling." I needed a physical-education class and it seemed an easy way to get that part of my haphazard degree plan behind me. I mean, how are you going to fail bowling?

As it would turn out, it was far and away the most interesting class I would take that semester.

Her name was Suzanne Levy. She had one of those smiles worth a million dollars, seemed friendly, and was about the best-looking classmate I'd ever had. I can't say much about her bowling ability.

I knew immediately that I was going to ask her out—just as soon as I got up the nerve.

"To be honest," says Suzanne, "I was only vaguely familiar with who Billy Olson was. I had read about him in the paper a time or two, but had never really paid that much attention to what he was doing with his pole vaulting.

"When he came into our bowling class and rolled about five strikes in a row, really showing everyone else up, I decided right away that he was a show-off. He kept saying he hadn't bowled since he was in high school, then he'd get another strike. And I couldn't even keep the ball out of the gutters.

"After a few days, though, we began to talk and finally he asked me out. Somehow, he found out that my birthday was on the day we were to have our first date, so he showed up with a rose for me.

"We went out and had a Coke and sat talking for a long time. Actually, he seemed very shy and had very little to say about himself. On the other hand, I wound up telling him my life story.

"I liked him, even if he was a better bowler than I was."

When I took Suzanne back to the dorm I thought maybe there would be a good-night kiss. After all, I'd brought a rose, hadn't I? No such luck. Then I suggested we go out again sometime soon. She didn't seem to respond to the idea.

It wasn't one of the shining moments in my romantic career. I told her good-night and decided I'd go back to concentrating on pole vaulting.

The indoor season had been a good one for me. I had gone to Dallas to talk with Dr. Pat Evans, the team doctor for the Dallas

Cowboys and one of the most highly regarded sports-medicine men in the country, about my leg injury, and he had given me a program that had helped a great deal. He changed the weight workouts I had been doing and suggested I get on a high-protein diet. If I was going to compete injury-free, he said, I was going to have to get stronger. And put on some weight. He advised that, instead of eating three meals a day at six-hour intervals, I try eating five times a day, hungry or not, for a while.

I felt as if I was spending half my waking hours eating, but by the time the indoor season got underway I had gained 15 pounds—up to 173—and was feeling stronger than ever before.

The only recommendation from Dr. Evans that really bothered me was that I vault wearing a long-legged girdle to support the muscle until I was certain my leg was back at full strength. Pro football quarterback Joe Namath may not have had any problems with wearing pantyhose in a television commercial some years back but, for me, going into a store and purchasing a women's girdle was no easy task.

The razzing I took in the dressing room wasn't much to brag about, either. But if that was what it took to get the leg well and me back to vaulting, I was not only ready, but willing.

I opened the indoor season with back-to-back wins in New York and Philadelphia, vaulting 17-9 and 17-10 respectively. In Ottawa, I cleared 17-9¾. Even in the meets where I lost, I was vaulting well.

Then at the Millrose Games in New York I pulled a hamstring muscle. It was a classic case of bad timing. The NAIA meet in Kansas City was just a week away, and the only real goal I had set for myself looked as if it was going to escape me. After winning the NAIA indoor and outdoor titles two years in a row, I decided it would be nice to complete my career with eight straight titles, something no one had ever done in the history of the Association. To win eight, however, I had to get number five. And since *walking* was enough of a problem after the New York meet, the prospects for winning didn't seem too bright.

Coach Hood, in fact, strongly recommended that I bypass the meet. Brad Pursley, vaulting well in his first season of competition for ACU, could probably win the event and get necessary points for the team. "The important thing for you to do," Coach Hood said, "is to get the leg well and start thinking about the outdoor season . . . and the Olympic Trials."

But by midweek I was moving around better and pursuaded Hood to allow me to make the trip with the rest of the team. I promised to vault only if the hamstring felt okay.

It never did, but I decided to vault anyway. I knew that even one jump would probably result in a reinjury of the hamstring, so I adopted an all-or-nothing game plan. First, I would have to convince Coach Hood that I had made a miracle recovery, then I would warm up slowly. When the bar got to a height that I felt would win the meet, I would take my one jump and see what happened.

"There's a very fine line you have to walk with pole vaulters," says Don Hood. "The last thing you want is for them to begin to fear vaulting. If an athlete is injured, you want him to get well as quickly as possible, because you won't want to have him idle so long that he begins to doubt himself, his abilities.

"In Billy's case, I felt strongly that he shouldn't vault. On the other hand, I knew how important it was to him to keep his string of national championships going.

"I've never known an athlete with the kind of competitive instinct he has. I think that's one of the reasons he's always come back from injuries so quickly—probably too quickly. But he's never going to change.

"He shouldn't have even been there that night in Kansas City. But he was, and what he did was amazing."

After the bar had been moved up to 17 feet, 6½ inches—the record height Olson had cleared the year before—the public address announcer informed those on hand that the defending champion would make his first attempt of the night.

A silence fell over the crowd as Olson, his injured leg heavily bandaged, moved slowly to the top of the runway and stood, staring at the bar.

Then there was a deep breath, an arching of the back to bring the pole into position. His run was not the smooth, almost effortless motion he had developed in recent years. Rather, it was a jerky, pained sprint. Clearly he was hurting.

Yet he managed to clear the height, to win his fifth championship, to keep the string of victories intact. He also injured the tender hamstring again—so badly that he was unable to walk to the winner's stand and receive his medal.

That was the end of the indoor season.

Despite the injury, the indoor season had given a big boost to my confidence. *Track & Field News* ranked me third in the United States behind Earl Bell and Jeff Taylor.

With some time between the end of the indoor season and the first outdoor meet, I felt confident the hamstring would be okay. Despite the fact that there were rumors President Carter might call for a U.S. boycott of the Olympic Games in protest of the Soviet Union's invasion of Afghanistan, there were few who felt politics would interfere with the chance for American athletes to compete in the Games. My outdoor season, then, would be geared toward peaking at the Olympics.

I thought back on that time Bob Richards had singled me out during one of his inspirational lectures, suggesting that I might one day be an Olympic competitor—maybe even a champion.

It became my goal to make his prophecy come true.

First, though, there was the matter of Suzanne Levy to settle. Since that first date we had seen each other only in class and occasionally on the campus. Badly as I wanted to, I could not bring myself to suggest another date for fear she would turn me down.

Finally, though, one afternoon when spring was in the air and the idea of sitting in a classroom less appealing than usual, she made the move I had been afraid to make. It was she who suggested we go for a drive and forget about class for the rest of the day.

It marked the beginning of a relationship which would have a dramatic effect on my life. A deeply committed Christian, she talked freely and easily about her faith in God and the comfort it provided her.

I think she viewed me as a free-spirited rabble-rouser, but she didn't force her own feelings about religion on me. To be honest, in times past I had felt more than a little uncomfortable around those who felt the need to preach a sermon, to flaunt their faith. But

Suzanne wasn't that way. She was simply a girl very comfortable with herself and her convictions.

I enjoyed being around her.

Another person I was enjoying being around was Brad Pursley, despite the fact that he was developing at such a rate that I knew full well I was going to have to stay on my toes just to remain the best vaulter at Abilene Christian.

One of those all-round athletes who had excelled at everything he tried in high school, he had come to ACU with thoughts of becoming a decathlon performer. But in his first year on campus he had shown such promise as a pole vaulter that Coach Hood and I had encouraged him to concentrate on it and forget the other events.

To this day I'm not at all sure it was a wise move on my part. At every meet in which we competed that spring, Brad was right there, nipping at my heels.

A sportswriter for the local paper even wrote a column suggesting the possibility that Abilene Christian might have two candidates for the Olympic team.

A native of Merkel, Texas, just a few miles outside Abilene, Brad Pursley had first seen Billy Olson when he was a sophomore in high school.

"I had gone to Abilene for a basketball tournament," he says, "and at one of the games someone pointed Billy out to me. He was a senior in high school then, and was winning a lot of meets. I couldn't believe what I saw. There was this skinny kid with long stringy hair down to his shoulders and his shirttail out, walking around like he was really something. If someone had asked me to give a description of a thug, I probably would have just pointed at Billy and said, 'There you are, the perfect example.'

"Which only goes to show you that first impressions shouldn't be taken too seriously. Little did I know I was talking about a guy who would become one of my very best friends.

"It was Billy, I later found out, who urged Coach Hood to recruit

me. He was the first one to really see that I had potential as a pole vaulter."

In time Brad and Billy would become close friends, working together toward common goals and gaining something of a Frick-and-Frack reputation on campus.

"We stay after each other all the time," Brad says. "Everything is a challenge, whether we're vaulting or riding motorcycles, water skiing or diving off those sixty-foot cliffs at Possum Kingdom Lake."

With that he launches into a series of yarns about their escapades.

There was the time, at an indoor meet in San Diego, when Billy was preparing to attempt a world record. Just before Olson was to vault, Pursley whispered in his ear that, if he made it, he would take off his shorts and run a fast lap around the track.

Billy made the height, but Brad was nowhere to be found. "He'd have tried to make me keep my word," Pursley says, "so I ducked into the dressing room and hid."

Then there was the posh post-meet party in Wichita at a local country club. "After the dinner Billy, Jeff Buckingham, Randy Hall, and I went outside and saw a golf cart parked near the clubhouse. Billy suggested a ride, and off we went into the night, touring the golf course. Suddenly, though, there were searchlights, and someone asking what we were doing.

"Billy was driving and quickly turned into the woods. Jeff and Randy jumped off the cart and started running back up to the dining room. Billy and I sat there, trying to decide whether we should run for it, too, or drive the cart back and take whatever was coming to us. We finally agreed that we couldn't just leave the cart out on the course.

"When we got back, there were a couple of security guards waiting for us. The first thing they asked us was our names.

"Billy, with this incredibly straight face, said, 'I'm Jeff Buckingham . . . and this is Randy Hall.'

"The guards wrote the names down and assured us our coaches would be hearing about what we'd done."

Theirs is not, however, a frivolous relationship. While there are fun times, both are highly dedicated to their pursuits of athletic excellence. And each has been good for the other.

"Anytime you have the chance to work with someone who is trying

*to achieve the same goals you are," Brad says, "it helps a great deal.
You see the other guy working hard, and that makes it easier for you
to work. Billy's a hard worker, and a great motivator.*

"He's helped me a great deal. And I like to think I've helped him."

There's no question that having Brad to work with helped me.
With him edging toward 18 feet, I found that I worked harder—
and was getting results.

At a meet in San Angelo, Texas, I cleared 18 feet, 7½ inches, the
third best in the world. And at the NAIA outdoor meet I won with a
clearance of 18-2 and had three good tries at a world-record 18-10.

The prospect of the Olympic Games fascinated me more and
more and became my driving force. Until President Carter made
the boycott official.

I was at the Texas Relays, getting ready to attempt a meet-
record 18 feet, 1½ inches, when I first heard that we definitely
would not send a team to Moscow. Like so many others, I simply
couldn't believe it. I was upset, for the simple reason that I had
come to feel I had a good chance of making the U.S. team.

Throughout the track-and-field community in the United
States, there was a general feeling of betrayal. Our reactions were
predictably self-centered at first. All the work and planning and
anticipation had been wiped away by a decision in the White House.

For a time many held to a glimmer of hope that the decision
would be reversed, that somehow all would be set right and the
United States would, in fact, be represented in Moscow.

But no such luck.

As I thought more about it and looked beyond my own personal
disappointment, I began to feel bad about many of my friends who
had been training for their last shot at making an Olympic team—
athletes who were nearing the ends of their careers but had decided to stay on a while longer just because of the Games.

Everywhere I competed thereafter I could sense that the enthusiasm for the season had diminished greatly. An air of excitement
and anticipation had been replaced with a "so what?" attitude.

Still, there would be Olympic Trials in Eugene, Oregon, and a
U.S. Olympic team would be named. While it would be all dressed
up with no place to go, there remained a certain degree of honor in

making the team. So I tried to keep the Trials as my number-one priority as the season went on.

I also managed to keep another goal in reach: winning the NAIA outdoor title—my sixth—so everything wasn't a loss.

As the summer approached I went into an inexplicable slump, failing to clear the opening height at the TAC national championships. But, then, just as suddenly as it had come, the slump was gone. The week before leaving for the Olympic Trials I had a couple of 18-6 jumps in practice—phenomenal for me—and left for Eugene confident, thinking I might not only earn one of the three spots on the team, but might also have a good chance of winning.

And Brad, who had upped his personal best to 18 feet, ½ inch, appeared to be in the running as well.

What greeted us on qualifying day was a cold morning rain that seemed to take the edge off the event for many on hand. Earl Bell, for instance, had made it from his home in Arkansas, but his poles hadn't. Using a borrowed pole, he failed to make the qualifying height of 17 feet, 2¾ inches. In fact, the list of those who failed to qualify for the finals sounded like a who's who of pole vaulting: Jeff Buckingham, Randy Hall, Joe Dial, Paul Pilla, and—unfortunately—Brad Pursley.

I was one of the 13 who qualified for the finals, which would be held after a day's rest.

Unlike the preliminaries, the finals were held on a gorgeous day, warm and sunny with a slight tailwind at the vaulters' backs. The conditions were ideal, and I'd never felt better.

During warmups I easily cleared 18-6 and was feeling good about my chances for the gold medal. And as the actual competition got underway, I got over 17-6 on my first attempt, then did the same at 18 feet.

By the time the bar reached 18-2½, there were five vaulters left in the competition. Mike Tully, Dan Ripley, and Tom Hintnaus (now vaulting for the University of Oregon) made it on their first attempts. Steve Smith cleared it on his third try.

And I missed all three times. On each vault I was six to eight inches over the bar but kept coming down into it, knocking it off. Coach Hood had urged me to move the standards forward, citing that as my problem, but I had been so confident I could make it I had ignored his advice.

What I did was choke. It was the first time I had ever done so in a major meet and it was a big disappointment to me. With something important at stake, I had failed to respond in the manner I should have.

Angry with myself, I sat and watched as Hintnaus cleared 18 feet, 4½ inches to win. Ripley and Tully tied for second, getting the other two spots on the team. Smith was fourth and I was fifth.

For Hintnaus, who had won on his home field, there was still the possibility of going on to Moscow. Born in Brazil, he had maintained dual citizenship and was thus eligible to vault for Brazil in the Olympics. Instead, he chose to honor the American boycott and bypass the opportunity.

Fortunately, I had little time to sit and brood over my disappointing performance at the Olympic Trials. The following day I flew to New York, then on to Europe, where I was to compete in a series of meets with members of the Pacific Coast Track Club.

For several months I had been trying to persuade Tom Jennings, Coach of the PCC, to allow me to become a member of his team, and finally he had agreed. I was thrilled because he had a reputation for being able to help pole vaulters get into really top-notch meets throughout the world. Besides, Bell, Tully, and Ripley were all members, so I felt as if I had gained admittance into a very exclusive group.

The European tour did a lot to help erase the none-too-pleasant memories of Eugene, Oregon.

I competed in eight meets and won seven of them, only finishing second in a meet in Stockholm. Twice, I competed against the Polish national champion, Wladyslaw Kozakiewicz, and defeated him—in a meet in Turku, Finland, then again in Milan, Italy.

Those wins would become particularly significant to me later in the summer when Kozakiewicz won the Olympic gold medal in Moscow with a jump of 18 feet, 11½ inches.

In Helsinki I set a stadium record, clearing 18 feet, 2½ inches. And on the island of Visby, just off the coast of Sweden, I went 18-4½.

The pole vault seemed to fascinate the people over there. I even did an exhibition at a Club Med resort. The owners had vaulting standards built on the volleyball court and stacked mattresses to serve as a landing pit. I was a bit nervous about the whole idea but managed to jump 17 feet, very nearly vaulting into a nearby tree that shaded the court.

All in all, the tour was a wonderful experience—not the Olympic Games, mind you, but fun. And it helped me mend my confidence.

Had I not come down with a galloping case of dysentery, which caused me to lose eight pounds in two days just before I was to return to the United States, I'd have given the trip a four-star rating.

One of the greatest things about competitive athletics, to me at least, is the fact that the victories and the defeats fade quickly. When one season is done, there is always another to look ahead to, promising improvement and new challenges.

Having rested for several weeks before enrolling in school again, I found myself more eager than ever to resume training.

I have never been good at remembering dates. Try though I might, I can't remember my mother's birthday. Or my dad's. Sometimes my own slips up on me.

But to this day, one date—29 September 1980—remains with me. It is almost as if a videotape were implanted in my brain. I can remember it all, just as if it happened in slow motion.

It was a day on which I thought my career as a pole vaulter had ended.

It was midafternoon on a Monday, and Brad Pursley and I were in the gymnastics room, going through a series of exercises we had been doing for several years.

One of our favorite routines was one wherein we would swing from a rope and go over a bar, simulating a vault. To get the necessary momentum, we had built a platform from which we would begin the swing. And, as with everything else Brad and I do, the exercise had turned into a form of competition.

Eventually, the platform was not high enough to provide the momentum we needed to get over new heights. We solved the problem by placing a chair on the platform and beginning our swing from it.

In time, we had advanced to climbing onto the rafters in the corner of the room. The longer arch of the swing provided us far greater height. As we would near the bar, the trick was to make the same kind of turn and push-off that one does when at the top of a vault. It was great fun and broke the monotony of running and lifting weights. But in retrospect I can see it had gotten out of hand. What was supposed to be a training exercise had become a daredevil kind of challenge.

Brad and I were both perched in the rafters, ready to make another swing. It was my turn to go first, and I began my swing with Brad telling me I'd better make it good because he was ready to show me some new trick he'd come up with.

The rope got me to the bar, I cleared it, I let go. And realized immediately I was in trouble. I had swung too far out and knew I was going to miss the protective padding that covered the cement floor.

Falling backwards, I turned to see where I was going to land and put my left arm out in an effort to cushion the fall as best I could.

As soon as I hit the floor a knifing pain shot through my arm. For a few seconds I thought I was going to black out. I lay still for a moment or two longer, then turned to see what damage had been done.

One's arm is at approximately a 90-degree angle when he's shaking hands. Mine was at that same angle, but in the opposite direction. And my wrist was broken in three places.

The pain and the sight of my disfigured arm sent a sick feeling through me. For some reason I still don't understand, I tried to put the arm back into place but couldn't. The elbow had been ripped completely out of its socket.

By the time the ambulance arrived, the elbow had swelled to three times its normal size and there was little feeling in my hand.

As I lay there, trying to be still, I kept thinking, *You've ruined everything. You're through. Ten minutes earlier you were an athlete on the way to something, maybe something big. Now you're nowhere, nothing.*

I was in the hospital six days. Most of that time was spent in anger—anger at the stroke of bad luck that had befallen me—and in wondering why. Never before or since have I felt such bitterness.

The anger was soon followed by depression.

The doctors had put the arm back in place with little difficulty and had advised my parents that it would, in all likelihood, be as good as new. The wrist was a different matter. One of the bones that had been broken was the one which controls most of the flexibility. It would heal, slowly, the doctors said, but there was a strong possibility it would never mend properly enough to withstand the strain of vaulting again.

I was ready to give up. But my friends weren't. Coach Hood and Brad kept telling me I would be back; they would help. But I wasn't hearing anything they had to say. My perspective was as out of place as the elbow had been.

Finally, it was an old friend, Frank Estes—someone who could identify with what I was going through—who came to the rescue. The injuries he had sustained in that fall in Waco had, by his own admission, destroyed his confidence and hurried his retirement from vaulting.

But Frank offered me no sympathy, nor did he bother to compare his situation to mine. "We're different people," he told me. "Most guys, me included, would use this as an excuse to hightail it out of sports. Everyone would understand. But you aren't that kind of person. You're the greatest competitor I've ever been around. You have to vault. You have to because you've got more talent and ability than almost any pole vaulter in the world.

"That's why you've got to quit acting like an idiot about this thing. Knowing you, if they had *amputated* the arm you would have tried to become the first one-handed pole vaulter in history. I know you, man. You've got to get well and get back to it. It won't be easy, but you'll make it."

I prayed to God that he was right.

It was in February that I finally went back to the track and started to run. I was weak and in terrible shape. After a few days, I got a pole from the equipment room. Even though my wrist was still in a cast, I wanted to see if I could vault.

That day I cleared 13 feet. It was a start. Maybe, just maybe, I could get in shape in time for the outdoor season. If so, I was going to dedicate it to a lot of people who had, thank the Lord, refused to allow me to give up on myself.

7

Arranging Priorities

OVER 200 STUDENTS *were crowded into the chapel on the Abilene Christian campus, listening to a young man who spoke easily and with a smile punctuating his every remark. Billy Olson, who had once sought ways to get out of attending the very service at which he was the guest speaker, was talking candidly to his peers of the importance of allowing God into their day-to-day lives.*

"Without Him, great performances, whether on the athletic field or in daily living, are all but impossible. Only through a strong belief in God can a person be assured a really successful life.

"What He wants from us," Billy continued, "is an honest effort to do the very best we can every day. And it isn't easy. I certainly don't always accomplish it, but it is my goal."

Speaking in a steady, even voice that had a strong ring of sincerity about it, he outlined for those on hand his five keys to living a good life:

1. Clean living;

2. Hard work;

3. Belief in one's self;

4. Refusal to accept failure, and the willingness to use it as a learning tool;

5. Assurance that God will help.

There were those who insisted that Billy's seemingly sudden interest in religion had come about as a result of his sobering accident that September day in the gymnastics room. Others gave girlfriend Suzanne Levy the credit for steering him toward the Bible and, ultimately, the church. Some, more skeptical, viewed him as just another in a lengthening line of "born-again" Christian athletes whose new conviction was subject to question.

But thoughts of a stronger commitment to a Christian life and the pursuit of a better understanding of the doctrine of the Church of Christ had been on Billy Olson's mind for some time. "I knew, as I said earlier, there was something missing in my life," he points out, "and I think I had known for quite some time what it was. At first I fought it, tried to ignore it. But there finally came a time when I could no longer pretend it wasn't there.

"At that point, I was faced with the problem of determining how to get started, how to make that first step in the direction of the church. That's where Suzanne helped. She began helping me with studying the Bible. And I had some long talks with Coach Hood.

"Mostly, though, I looked inside myself and realized that I could be a better person, that there was more to life than being a pretty-good pole vaulter. I wanted to be more than that. I wanted to be a Christian. And, as with almost everything else good that's ever happened in my life, there were a lot of people standing by, eager to help."

And then he thought of a way to repay that friendly assistance. Once an admittedly selfish person, he began to reach out to others more than he had ever done in his life.

Though once not comfortable speaking to groups, he went to Coach Hood and suggested that he would like to have the opportunity to talk with youngsters, to share some of his new found feelings. Maybe, he said, he could help them avoid some of the dead-end pursuits he had chased in his teenage days.

It is impossible to describe the frustration I felt that winter when the indoor season got into full swing. A year in which I had strongly felt I could threaten records and maybe establish myself as the best vaulter in the United States was threatening to be a year in which the athletic world would simply forget about Billy Olson.

At the end of the 1980 outdoor season I had been ranked tenth in the world. And now I was being labeled a has-been. There were those, I knew, who were suggesting I would never vault again.

I knew I would, but I had no idea how well. The elbow would be no problem, but the wrist might. As it slowly healed, I found that I had very little flexibility in it. I could not bend my hand up or down as I once had.

Frankly, I was concerned about the stress the wrist would undergo when I really tried to go full speed into a vault. But I had made up my mind to give it an honest effort. If things didn't work out, I didn't want it to be because I didn't try.

While I tried to rehabilitate and to get back into shape that winter, Brad was flying the Abilene Christian colors well. He managed to clear 17 feet, 9 inches and ended the season as the number-one-ranked vaulter in the U.S. I was pleased for him, but found his success frustrating as well. I wanted to be able to challenge him for that ranking!

Maybe, I kept telling myself, the year could be salvaged when the outdoor season got underway.

It was May before I felt confident enough to see how I might fare in competition. Accepting an invitation to the Pepsi Invitational in Los Angeles, I arrived at the meet more nervous than I can ever remember being before a competition. With great difficulty, I managed to clear 17 feet—and finished seventh. It wasn't exactly a glorious comeback, but the wrist held up. It was a start.

The performance provided me with an awareness of several things I had not previously had answers for. One, I was going to be okay physically. Two, I had not been hesitant about jumping. But the third thing bothered me a lot. I simply was not in the kind of shape necessary to compete against the top vaulters in the country. And I wasn't sure there was time enough left in the season to gain the sharpness I needed.

All I could do was go back home and work as hard as I could. I knew I had a lot of catching up to do, but I just might be able to make it. The European season would stretch into the summer. If I could do well enough in the late stages of the U.S. season, maybe I would get a chance to vault abroad. And in Europe in the summer I might be able to vault well enough to prove I was still in the hunt.

It was on the final day of May that things began looking up. At the TFA-USA Outdoor Championships in Wichita, I cleared 18 feet for the first time since my accident.

There were 38 vaulters in the field, and the large number of contestants caused the competition to drag on for five hours. Finally the field was narrowed to Earl Bell and me. We both got over 18 feet, ¼ inch. Earl won on fewer misses, but I felt more encouraged than I had in some time.

I called home to tell Mom and Dad how I'd done. Mom, of course, was more interested in how my wrist and elbow felt than in the fact I had placed second. But when I told Dad that I had cleared 18 feet again he obviously was thrilled. "Son," he said, "I knew you could do it. What you've been able to do this year is really amazing. I'm proud of you."

That made the day complete.

The day before the TAC Championships in Sacramento, word came that Thierry Vigneron, the top vaulter in France, had established a new world record in a meet in Macon, France. He had cleared 19 feet, ¼ inch, thus becoming the first man in history to break the 19-foot barrier.

He had accomplished what had become a private goal of mine. At the end of the 1980 season, I had begun to think about clearing 19 feet, dreaming of becoming the first to do it. That's one of the accomplishments to which track-and-field athletes aspire—pioneering in their chosen event. People will forever remember that it was Roger Bannister who first broke through the four-minute-mile barrier and that Parry O'Brien was the first shot putter to get beyond 60 feet. I had hoped it would be Billy Olson who was the first to get over 19.

Now, however, the task was to play catch-up; which was rather ambitious thinking for a vaulter who had only cleared 18 feet and had yet to win his first meet of the season.

That would change the following day in the brain-baking heat of Sacramento. With the temperature well over 100 degrees, I won the first TAC title of my career, clearing 18 feet, 2½ inches.

And, had the circumstances been different, I think I might have been able to return home as the American record holder.

After I cleared the winning height, Steve Smith, who had one miss already, passed. We decided to move the bar up to 18 feet, 6½ inches. I waited while he took more than 30 minutes to make his two attempts at the height.

Suffering from a tight hamstring, he stalled for time in every way he could. First, he persuaded officials that he needed a different pole to use at the height and went off in search of it. He returned to say that the shed in which the other pole was stored had been locked and he could not find a key. Then he made several runs down the runway to test his leg.

All the while the momentum I had built up was slipping away. When he did finally make two unsuccessful jumps at the height, I knew I was no longer mentally prepared to go for the record. I tried 18 feet, 8¾ inches but didn't make it.

I left the competition with mixed feelings. I had won my first major outdoor title, and in doing so I had earned a spot on the United States team that would compete in the World Cup meet in Rome later in the summer. On the other hand, I couldn't help feeling that Smith's delay tactics had robbed me of a legitimate chance at the American record.

As reports continued to filter in from Europe, it became more and more important to me to try for new heights. In June, the Soviet Union's Vladimir Polyakov improved on Vigneron's new world mark, clearing 19 feet, ¾ inch. Then, just a few days later, Konstantin Volkov, yet another Russian vaulter, cleared an incredible 19 feet, 2 inches. Volkov's mark would not be ratified by the records committee because it had come in a meet that was not, according to the news reports, up to the standards of the International Amateur Athletic Federation. But, ratified or not, it was a performance that earned everyone's attention.

Clearly, a vault in the neighborhood of 19 feet was going to be necessary soon if the U.S. was to keep pace with the rest of the world. And since I was still not in the kind of condition I felt was necessary to count on any manner of consistency, I made a decision that was to put me squarely in the center of a summer controversy.

Most of the American qualifiers for the World Cup team were to spend a month competing in various meets in Europe before gathering in Rome. I badly wanted to go to Europe with them, but decided the time would be better spent staying at home, working myself into better condition.

It was not a decision that set well with a man named Jim Tuppeny, the track coach at the University of Pennsylvania, who had been selected as the head coach for the U.S. World Cup team. He made it clear that I should be in Europe, competing on a regular basis, proving to him that I was fit and deserving of the place I had earned on the team.

He was an easy man to dislike.

As Billy battled back from his injury to return to competition, Coach Don Hood silently marveled at the spirit of the young man he was coaching. It was the determination he saw that convinced him, beyond any doubt, that his young protégé would soon emerge as one of the finest pole vaulters in the world.

"And," Hood says, "I knew that with that recognition would come a number of new things to deal with. I thought for a long time about what to say to him, what kind of advice to give him. Finally, I sat down one night and wrote him a long letter.

"Basically, I told him that he was developing into the kind of athlete people all over the world were going to be watching very carefully. I tried to point out to him the fact that he could serve as a very positive influence on a lot of people. Aware that he was beginning to take an interest in his spiritual well-being, I urged him to pursue it with even more enthusiasm. And, if he was serious in his desire to speak with youth groups, he should get into a speech class and work on his grammar.

"In a way, I was hard on him in the letter, pointing out some of the shortcomings which I was concerned that people would begin to pick at once he became a more public figure. But they were criticisms with positive intent. I had always thought of Billy as a fine young man, from the first time I met him back when he was in high school. But, on the other hand, I saw so much unused potential. I felt it my responsibility as his coach, and as his friend, to point that out."

The criticisms and advice were taken to heart. In time, Billy approached Hood about making a more sincere commitment to becoming a Christian. "He wanted to study the Bible, and talked of being baptized into the Church of Christ. So we began to have long talks in the evening. I gave him some materials to study and provided what insight I could.

"And I repeatedly pointed out that he be careful not to go into the

matter half-heartedly. I knew Suzanne had had a tremendously positive effect on him, but I wanted him to be certain that he was not making this kind of commitment for her benefit. Or for mine.

"Too, there were some problems he had to work out with his parents. Members of the Baptist denomination, they were at first skeptical about his decision to join the Church of Christ. That worried him a great deal, knowing how strongly his parents felt about their own religious convictions."

Throughout the spring Billy wrestled with his decision, all the while talking with friends, teammates, his coach and his girlfriend about their Christian involvement.

Then one afternoon following practice he sought Coach Hood out and asked a favor of him. "I would like to be baptized," he said, "and I would like for you to be the one to baptize me."

"Of all the wonderful experiences I've had in sports," Hood says, "there has never been anything to compare to the feeling I had the evening I baptized Billy. It was, as I told him, something that was forever. In time all the trophies and medals and write-ups would fade and be gone for both of us. But that night was the beginning of something he would carry with him for the rest of his life."

Suzanne Levy had witnessed the change in Billy at closer range than anyone. "I could see it coming," she says, "but I just didn't know when. After his accident, he had become more serious about a lot of things. It was as if he had developed a new perspective. The most noticeable thing was the manner in which he demonstrated concern for other people. I think he realized that others had done so much for him for so long that maybe he needed to return the favors.

"I remember a couple of athletes in school who were getting pretty involved in drugs. Billy sought them out and talked with them, reminding them of how important they were and how they were taking a chance of throwing away a great deal. These people didn't come to Billy for advice; he just went to them. And he helped them get their lives straightened out.

"When we first started talking about teaching a youth group, he went to Coach Hood, concerned that he wasn't qualified, wasn't enough of a Bible scholar, to be working with kids like that. For-

tunately, Coach Hood convinced him that he needed only to be honest with the kids.

"And they loved him from the very beginning. Because he's such a motivator and such an honest person, they hung on his every word. It was an amazing thing to watch. He was like a Pied Piper to them. And he realized the responsibility of the role.

"I don't think he has any idea how many kids he's helped over the years. But then, he's not the kind of person who would keep score, anyway."

I *was* keeping score of the number of vaulters around the world who were jumping much higher than I was. If I was to prove that I belonged in their company, it was essential that I make a good showing at the World Cup meet, which is the closest thing to the Olympic Games in a non-Olympic year.

In the World Cup meet, every country is represented by only one performer in each event (unlike the Olympics, to which each country sends three athletes per event). Thus the pole-vault field at the World Cup would represent the absolute cream of the crop. And so I went to work, doubling up to catch up. I knew there was no way I could be in peak shape for the competition, but I was going to try to be in as good shape as possible. Then, with a little luck, maybe I could give the European vaulters a run for their money.

Jim Tuppeny, however, had already made up his mind that I couldn't. He had made it clear that he wanted to replace me on the team with Earl Bell, who had been vaulting well for several weeks in meets in Europe.

Learning of his plan when I arrived in Brussels, I was livid. I had heard he had already contacted Earl about vaulting in Rome.

Admittedly, Earl had been jumping well, and he had made it clear to Tuppeny that he would like the opportunity to compete in the World Cup. At the same time, he pointed out that I had, in fact, earned the position by winning the TAC meet.

At the meet in Brussels I cleared 17-8 and placed fourth. I was reasonably pleased with my effort, particularly since I had been quite rusty. Tuppeny, however, wasn't impressed and informed me that he was taking me off the team.

I told him, in a manner which, frankly, wasn't all that Christian, that I had earned the right to be on the team and planned to compete. Finally, after several heated discussions, he backed down some. If I vaulted well in the practice sessions leading up to the World Cup, I could remain on the U.S. team.

I had no other choice. What had been planned as an enjoyable trip (my mother and Suzanne had accompanied me) had turned into a nightmare. It angered me to have to prove myself—in essence to earn my place on the team—a second time. The joy of being a part of the United States team had gone out of the experience.

Finally, just days before the competition was scheduled to begin, I learned that I would be jumping in the World Cup meet.

The third annual World Cup meet was held in the same stadium in which the 1960 Olympics had been held. The Russian, Volkov, proved to everyone that his 19-2 jump had been no fluke, winning the gold medal with a vault of 18 feet, 8¼ inches. Jean-Michel Bellot of France, who had made the team ahead of Vigneron, was second at 18-2½. And I finished third, earning the bronze medal with a jump of 18 feet, ½ inch.

Considering everything that had happened—the injury, missing much of the season, the flap with Tuppeny—I felt it was a very respectable performance.

I felt I had proven myself. I wasn't the best by any stretch of the imagination. But I was among the best. And I felt confident that there would be better days ahead.

Mom, Suzanne, and I left for home immediately. There would be time for a couple of weeks' rest, then it would be back to school and preparation for the upcoming indoor season.

While I would not be ranked in the world's top ten vaulters for 1981, I felt I had managed to salvage the season. It would provide a good springboard to 1982.

As the indoor season neared, I was more anxious to get back into competition than I could ever remember being. As my workouts continued to go well, I called Tom Jennings several times to let him know I was anxious to vault in every meet he could get me into. He said he would make the arrangements. On most weekends, in fact, I would be vaulting in one meet on Friday night and another on Saturday. That was fine with me.

I had hoped to open the season with a fast start, but I had not expected the turn of events that transpired at the Vitalis-Olympic Invitational in New York. There, in the first meet of the season, I cleared 18 feet, 6½ inches to set a new American indoor record.

Suddenly, I was in a position of at least attempting a new world record at virtually every meet in which I competed. I won the Philadelphia Classic for the third straight year, clearing 18 feet, ½ inch, then had three unsuccessful attempts at 18-6¾. The very next night I waited until the bar went to 18-1 before entering the competition at the TFA-USA Indoor Championships in Wichita. I made it on my second try, then tried once again to push the record a half-inch above the mark I'd set in New York. Once again, I failed, but I felt certain I was going to go higher before long.

The *Toronto Star*-Maple Leaf Games officials called to advise me they were making the pole vault their featured event. Vigneron, making one of his rare appearances outside of France, had agreed to compete. They were billing it as a head-to-head battle between the French national record holder and the American record holder. Members of the media, in fact, were suggesting that a world mark might result.

A sellout crowd was on hand for the January 29 meet, and there was little doubt the pole vault was one of the main things they had come to see. There was an electricity in the arena that gave the whole evening a circus atmosphere. I loved it.

I decided to wait until the bar had been raised to 18 feet, ½ inch before entering the competition. I made it on my first jump. Vigneron also cleared, as did Earl Bell and Dave Volz.

Then, at 18-4½, I again cleared on my first attempt. Vigneron missed on each of his attempts and was out. But the competition was far from over.

When the bar went to 18-6½—the record height I'd cleared earlier in the month—both Earl and Volz, the sophomore from the University of Indiana, made it.

It was cat-and-mouse time. Having felt so good on my first two jumps of the night, I decided to pass at the height and go for the world record.

The almost constant roar of the crowd which is a part of indoor track and field fell to a churchlike hush as I prepared to take my first jump at 18 feet, 8¾ inches. I was aware of competitors in other events stopping to watch as the public address announcer informed everyone that I was attempting a world indoor record.

Everything seemed to go perfectly. My run was good, the pole plant just as I wanted. I cleared the bar with ease as the crowd burst into applause. Finally, I had a world record, and it was a great feeling.

The bonus which accompanied it was the fact that Earl and Dave had both vaulted well, pushing Vigneron into fourth place. For some time there had been criticism that American vaulting had fallen behind the rest of the world. That night in Toronto we began catching up.

The following evening in Dallas, Vigneron withdrew and returned to France. Tired and a little drained by the excitement of the night before, I still managed to clear 18 feet, ½ inches, beating my friend Brad Pursley on fewer misses.

Pole vaulting, however, is far from being an exact science. Even when you're on a hot streak, there are always things that can go wrong. The following Friday night at the *Los Angeles Times* meet was a good example. The new world-record holder flopped in grand style, failing to clear the opening height.

Hoping for better things the following evening, I took a late flight out of L.A. and, along with Earl and Brad, headed for Louisville and the Mason-Dixon Indoor Games. The jokes we had made in Los Angeles International about the chances of our poles arriving at the same destination to which we were headed for didn't seem quite as funny on arrival. Mine made it, but for some strange reason Earl's and Brad's were enroute to Philadelphia.

Early in the competition at the Louisville Convention Center, one might have thought I also was vaulting with a borrowed pole. It took me three jumps to clear the opening height of 17-6, and when I did it wasn't anything to write poems about. Then I managed 18 feet on my second attempt, still looking like anything but a world-record holder.

Brad and Earl, jumping with my poles, had even worse luck, and the 18-foot jump assured me of the win. Then, still uncertain that I was capable of threatening any records, I told officials to move the bar up just 4½ inches. It would serve as a test. If I could make that, then maybe I would take another crack at the record.

Frankly, I was a bit surprised when I did finally clear the height on my third attempt. What the heck, I might as well keep going. The officials moved the bar to 18 feet, 9¼ inches.

And, lo and beyond, on my third attempt I cleared it by a mile. I had nudged the world record up another inch.

Two weeks later I broke the record for a third time. It was in the Jack-in-the-Box Invitational in San Diego that I cleared 18 feet, 9½ inches.

Following the competition, reporters kept asking what had prompted the string of record-setting jumps, what had brought about the marked improvement. I pointed to Earl, who was sitting nearby. "That guy over there is probably the biggest reason. Every weekend we've been going at it tooth and nail. If I'm going to beat him, I've got to vault at record heights."

The next night in San Francisco, Earl proved my point. He cleared 18-4½ to win, and I could do no better than 18 feet, ½ inch. He had also beaten me the week before at the Millrose Games in Madison Square Garden. I might have been the owner of the world record, but there was never any night when I felt certain I was going to win.

Officials of the indoor TAC-Mobil National Championships had pursuaded Vigneron to return to the U.S. for one more meet, and had even invited several legendary vaulters to be on hand to witness the competition. There was Cornelius Warmerdam, the first man ever to clear 15 feet and the one who had inspired my first backyard vaults back on Lexington Avenue, and John Uelses, the first man to vault over 16 feet.

That night I cleared 18 feet, 6½ inches to win, and Earl was second at 18-2½. Vigneron was third.

In addition to earning the national indoor championship, Billy was the recipient of the Mobil Grand Prix overall winner's prize: $7,000 earned for accumulating the greatest number of points in specified meets during the season. By winning nine of the 13 meets in which he had competed, he also won the $3,000 award which went to the top point-maker in the pole vault.

Viewed by athletes as one of the greatest advancements in the sport of track and field, the Grand Prix prizes are given in an attempt to help men and women continue their training past collegiate eligibility. The Athletics Congress (TAC), in approving the prize-money format, ruled that amateur rules would not be violated so long as it was allowed to manage trust funds for the athletes earning the money. TAC would then provide the athletes with funds for living and training expenses.

For Billy there would be one other award, one which carried no cash prize but a great deal of prestige. Track & Field News *named him its Indoor Athlete of the Year.*

But there was one more item of business to be tended before he would consider the winter a success. The night after the TAC indoor championships, Billy was in Kansas City, hoping to win his seventh NAIA vaulting title.

The meet was important to me for a number of reasons. First, of course, was the fact that I was in my final year of eligibility and was getting close to accomplishing my goal of winning both the NAIA indoor and outdoor championships four times. A win in what was to be my final collegiate indoor meet would get me halfway there.

And, too, there was once again the very real possibility that ACU vaulters could finish in the top four spots.

I was tired from the late-night flight from New York and went to the arena with no thought of breaking records. The important thing, for me and for the team, was to win. Anything beyond that would simply be icing on the cake.

Again I had difficulties early in the competition, finally getting over 17 feet but not looking too stylish in doing so. Then I managed 18-2½ and was assured the win I so badly wanted.

Brad Pursley, clearing 17 feet, was second, Dale Jenkins was third, and Bobby Williams, fourth. We had our sweep.

And before the night was over I had improved on the world record for the fourth time during the season. With Coach Hood and Brad urging and coaching, I decided to have a try at 18-10.

On my third attempt I made it, bringing the indoor season to the kind of ending you dream about but wouldn't dare believe could actually happen.

It would be nice to get home and get some rest before turning my thoughts to outdoor vaulting.

In truth, I am much like the old firehouse dog. He hears the alarm and he's off, chasing the fire engine. When I hear there's a track meet, my first thought is to pack my bags and to check plane schedules. I've often been criticized for competing too much, for not taking the month or six weeks off between the indoor and outdoor season that many vaulters do.

To me, the prospect of competition is magnetic. And fun. But this time I made myself an unbreakable promise that I was going to take a little time off and give my body a rest. A month, I figured, would do nicely.

I kept my word for almost a week.

First, there was a meet on the ACU campus and I jumped only 17-6 before ending what amounted to a good workout. (A sudden storm cancelled the meet before I could try any higher.) Then, on 20 March, we traveled to nearby Brownwood for the Bluebonnet Relays, a meet in which I'd been participating since high school days.

There I vaulted to a new American outdoor record, clearing 18 feet, 8¾ inches. Clearing the height on my second attempt, I added a half-inch to the existing record which Dave Roberts had established at the 1976 Olympic Trials. Someone with a real nose for trivia also did some research and found that it was the earliest in the season an American record had been set in the pole vault since 1926, when someone named Lee Barnes had upped the mark to 13 feet, 5¼ inches.

I wasn't sure what to make of it all. Had the momentum I had built during the indoor season simply carried over to the outdoor campaign? Did that mean there might be a slump sometime later in the spring? Or was it a signal of even better things to come as the spring and summer went on? I chose to assume the latter.

The possibility of vaulting 19 feet became a fascination with me. At Brownwood, in fact, I attempted the height. I was close, but it was still early. In time, I was sure, it would come.

What was to come more immediately was a series of record-setting performances by jumpers all over the United States.

Aside from a couple of meets where I no-heighted, I enjoyed a near-perfect season until the middle of May, when I lost to a fast-improving Dave Volz at the Pepsi International. He cleared 18-4½ to my 18 feet, ½ inch.

The following week, however, the defeat was quickly forgotten as I went 18-3 to win the NAIA outdoor title. That was number eight, and I don't think I would have felt any better had I gone 19 feet. By winning, I had ended a pursuit which had, because of the year's layoff due to the injury, taken five years to accomplish. Even today it ranks as one of the accomplishments I'm most proud of.

I came down out of the clouds pretty quickly a week later, when Dan Ripley emerged as a real challenger, winning the TFA title with a vault of 18 feet, 6¾ inches. I was second.

Then came word from Juarez, Mexico, of all places, that Larry Jessee had tied my American record. Frankly, the news raised eyebrows throughout the vaulting fraternity. A former student at the University of Texas at El Paso, Jessee seemed to always come up with his outstanding jumps there on the UTEP campus. Get him out of El Paso, and he didn't seem to be the same vaulter you had read about in the paper.

Aware of the criticisms, he told reporters he was really thrilled to finally vault well somewhere other than in El Paso. I found his statement amusing, since the track in Juarez where he had tied the record was right across the border from El Paso, only a short cab ride from the UTEP campus.

Still, officially I was no longer sole owner of the American record. And, barring a trip to El Paso, I didn't expect to get the opportunity to go head-to-head with Jessee.

Frankly, I had other people who worried me a great deal more. One was my Pacific Coast Club teammate Ripley. In effect, he had beaten me twice already, since he was the winner at the Mt. San Antonio College Invitational where I had no-heighted earlier in the season. And, at age 28, he was vaulting better than I'd ever seen him.

At the TAC-Mobil outdoor national championships, he looked great. And I started off like someone just learning the sport. I needed all three jumps to make the qualifying height of 17 feet, 4½ inches while he just breezed along, screaming over the early heights.

Finally, though, I seemed to get into the proper groove, and we turned the event into a two-man battle. In time the bar went up to the new American record height of 18 feet, 9¼ inches, and we both went over.

Suddenly the name of Larry Jessee was wiped from the record books, and it was Dan and me at the top of the list. But only for a while.

A week later, in a meet in Durham, North Carolina, Dave Volz replaced both of us, clearing 18 feet, 9½ inches in a triangular meet involving the United States, West Germany, and a team from the Pan-African nations.

I should, perhaps, point out here that a remarkable underground network exists in the pole-vaulting world. Regardless of where an outstanding performance occurs, you can bet that, within a matter of hours, vaulters everywhere will know what the weather conditions were, what brand of pole was used, and how the vaulter looked making the height he achieved.

The word on Dave's record vault was that once again he had successfully used a technique that had been named after him— "volzing." In what I must admit is an amazing display of agility and quick thinking, he had, on numerous occasions, "saved" an obviously missed jump by using a hand or arm to keep the bar in place. In Durham, the word was, the bar had bent down almost six inches as he tried to get over, yet had amazingly stayed in place.

Earl Bell, a guy who learned to speak his piece growing up in Arkansas, was the most outspoken about the matter. "The rules of pole vaulting," he said, "are very simple. You either clear the bar, or you don't. Obviously Volz didn't."

Statements like Earl's—and mine about Larry Jessee—probably have a strong sour-grapes ring to them. Such, I can assure you, is not the case. What you have to understand is that there is a very jealous guarding of the integrity of the event. I know of no other athletic pursuit in which competitors are so quick to applaud another's outstanding performance. On the other hand, there is no hesitation to cry "foul" when there is the feeling that one has been committed.

I looked forward to going up against Volz as much as I did competing against Soviet vaulters who were coming for a U.S.-U.S.S.R. dual meet on the Fourth-of-July weekend. It would be the final major meet of the U.S. outdoor season, and it would provide yet another opportunity for us to convince the rest of the world that American vaulting was ready to meet what the newspapers had been calling a European assault.

Vigneron of France had not fared well during the indoor season. Now it was time to see how the highly regarded Soviet vaulters would do.

The meet was held in Indianapolis with all the pomp and circumstance that generally accompany an international competition. That it was a meet pitting the United States against the Russians made it even more special. The American boycott of the Moscow Olympic Games was still relatively fresh on everyone's mind, and the reporters were having a field day. In essence they were saying, "Okay, now the Soviets will get a chance to see what kind of competition they were spared last summer."

Vaulting for the U.S.S.R. were Vladimir Polyakov, Konstantin Volkov, and Viktor Spasov. (Spasov was actually the alternate on the team. He would be allowed to vault, but his points would not be counted in the team totals.) Competing for the United States were Volz and myself.

As I prepared for the meet I couldn't help but think back on that U.S.-U.S.S.R. junior meet years earlier. It had been a day on which I wasn't supposed to even seriously challenge the Soviet vaulters, yet I had won. That meet, in truth, was the one which had provided my first shot of real confidence.

There is a special feeling that comes from beating the best the Soviet Union has to offer. I'm sure some of the motivation is based on the fact that we're political enemies. However, I believe it comes more from the awareness that their athletes are among the best.

I can't remember many times when I've looked forward to a competition as much as I did that dual meet in Indianapolis.

In the early going I found myself wondering if it was a fair fight. Volz failed to clear the opening height and was out of the running before things really even heated up. And each of the Soviet vaulters looked outstanding during warmups.

Volkov, however, had his problems as the actual competition got underway and could clear only 17 feet, 3½ inches. When we got to 18-1¼, the contest was among Spasov, Polyakov, and me. We all made the height.

When the bar went to 18-3¼, I went over with relative ease, then sat to watch the Russians try. After another 30 minutes the competition was over. Both had failed at the height and would share second place. For the first time in many years, they had been defeated in international competition and I would be hiding behind false modesty to say I wasn't thrilled.

Records are nice, but winning over a highly regarded competitor is something else again.

Feeling more confident than I had at any point in the season, I left for a summer in Europe, hoping to get a chance to meet the ever-growing list of French vaulters who were recording outstanding heights. But at the same time, I felt no alarming sense of urgency. Both indoors and out, I felt, I had proven myself.

I made up my mind that I was going to enjoy my stay in Europe. And if I vaulted well, so much the better.

Exhausted by the trip and the time change, my first week was a competitive disaster. It was as if every ounce of energy had been drained from my body. In the first three meets I entered, I failed to make the opening height.

It was time to fall back and regroup. I decided to go back home and spend a couple of weeks just training, getting my technique back to where I felt it should be. By the time I returned to Europe in mid-August, things had come together and I had won six straight meets at heights ranging from 18-4½ to 18-8¾.

It was mid-September before I headed for home. The long season, one which had begun back in January, was finally over.

But it had been worth every bumpy airline trip, every lost pole and uncomfortable hotel bed. When all was said and done, I had gone over 18 feet, 4½ inches in 19 meets, had defeated each of the top-ranked vaulters I competed against, and had enjoyed an almost injury-free year.

Even the fact that Volz, also touring Europe, had improved the American record to 18 feet, 10¼ inches in a meet in Nice, France failed to dim the positive feelings I had about the just-finished season.

When the world rankings for the year were announced, I was finally number one. It was the first time there had been an American leader since 1976. Dave Volz was second, followed by the Russians and Jean-Michel Bellot of France. Dan Ripley, despite an unfortunate bout with hepatitis which prevented his competing in Europe, ranked sixth.

The next stop for me, I hoped, would be 19 feet. I wasn't certain enough to predict that it would come—as it did—at the *Toronto Star*-Maple Leaf Indoor Games that following February, but I knew I was capable of getting there.

When I did, I felt a great rush of relief. But, as always seems to be the case in sports, no sooner is one goal achieved than another is set. If I could set a world record indoors, why not outdoors as well?

8

The Crowded Sky

AS THE 1983 INDOOR SEASON came to a close, Billy Olson had clearly emerged as one of the most dominant figures in his sport. Three times in a matter of months he had improved the world indoor record, finally boosting it beyond the major 19-foot mark. He had again claimed the gold medal at the U.S.A. Indoor Championships in Madison Square Garden and won the Mobil Grand Prix overall men's title for the second year in a row.

The latter accomplishment added $13,000 to his trust fund, which was being administered by The Athletics Congress.

Olson's boyish enthusiasm and easygoing Texas manner had captured the attention of the media throughout the country. As his vaults had gone higher and higher, so had interest in this athlete, who was now being regarded as the odds-on favorite to claim the pole-vault gold medal at the 1984 Olympic Games in Los Angeles. Suddenly he was the subject of stories in Sports Illustrated, Time, People, and Family Weekly. Newspaper journalists from Los Angeles to New York sought him out to learn more about him and his event.

For the first time since Don Bragg, the 1960 Olympic champion who fascinated fans with his Tarzan yells during competition, an American pole vaulter was a bona fide national hero.

Letters addressed simply to "Billy Olson, Pole Vaulter" were finding their way to his mailbox, seeking autographed pictures, asking advice, and wishing him well in his Olympic bid.

Somewhat to his surprise, Olson had become something more than an athlete. In a time when the sports-page headlines rang out *stories of professional football player strikes, ill-mannered tennis players, drug scandals, and demands for bank-breaking salaries, stories of the achievements and pursuits of a young amateur athlete from the hinterlands of West Texas were refreshing relief.*

The kid who started out with the piece of bamboo pole in the backyard had grown into a full-blown celebrity.

The publicity wasn't all helpful to Billy's hometown image—or even true. "When a writer from Sports Illustrated *mentioned that Billy's favorite beer was a particular brand brewed in Canada,*" *says* Abilene Reporter-News *sportswriter Bill Hart,* "I really didn't think much about it. But there were a lot of people in Abilene who went into shock. You have to understand we're a pretty conservative group of people. I'm not saying we don't have our share of beer drinkers, but folks around here keep things like that pretty quiet.

"It turned out that Billy had been talking with a writer who was drinking a Molson's beer and had said something like, 'That's got to be a great beer. It even has my name in it.' So, the story comes out saying that's his favorite brand. Before it was all over, Sports Illustrated got several calls from folks here in Abilene pointing out in no uncertain terms that Billy Qlson didn't drink Molson's or any other kind of beer."

Among those calling was Billy himself.

The celebrity status was, on one hand, pleasing. If nothing else, it was tangible evidence of Olson's athletic progress. On the other hand, it was a strange, discomforting situation to be in. With requests to speak, to do television appearances, and attend pole-vaulting clinics and competitions in every remote part of the world, he found himself, for the first time in his life, in a position of having to say no.

It was simply impossible to do everything everyone wanted him to do.

"Billy," *says Don Hood,* "is one of those people who wakes up believing there are going to be 28 hours in every day. He thinks he can manage to get everything done, regardless of how full his schedule might be.

"In the past couple of years in particular, he's found himself in several roles. He's a world-class athlete, of course, with the obligations of training and competing. Then, because of his success, he's *something of a spokesman for his sport. The publicity he receives generates interest in pole vaulting, and he feels a strong obligation in that regard.*

"Then, there's his Christian witness. He realizes now that he is also a role model for a lot of youngsters.

"Last summer, we were having a track meet in Abilene—just an informal summer meet—and Billy agreed to compete in the pole vault. And, since the meet started late in the afternoon, he was concerned that the event might run so long that he would be late for an evening speaking engagement he had.

"I assumed it must be some big deal, some kind of awards banquet or something. As it turned out, he was to address the youth group at a Church of Christ in nearby Miles, Texas. But it was obviously important to him that he be there to talk with the kids.

"Well, the vault ran late, just as he had feared it would. No sooner had he made his final jump than he ran for his car, still wearing his warmup uniform.

"But in his haste to get to where he was supposed to be, he had a minor accident even before he got outside the city limits. He was far less upset about the damage to his car than he was about missing the meeting he was supposed to attend. Even before calling a wrecker to come tow his car to the garage, he found a pay phone and placed a call to the head of the FCA group, explained his situation, apologized, and promised to make it the next week.

"And he did. To me, that's the kind of thing that makes Billy Olson a special person."

In years past, I had ended the indoor season exhausted, suffering from mindless jet-lag brought on by coast-to-coast travel and participating in two meets a weekend. As a result, I had found myself going into the outdoor season drained.

To avoid that mistake, I made up my mind to take a couple of months off to rest, train, and prepare myself for what I felt certain was going to be the best outdoor year I'd ever had. I wanted to break the outdoor world record, and I was keenly aware that the '83 season would provide me an opportunity to prove that the number one ranking I had enjoyed the previous season was valid.

In August the first-ever World Track and Field Championships would be held in Helsinki, Finland. In a sense, it would be like a dress rehearsal for the Olympic Games a year early. And the winner there would gain a tremendous edge as the summer Games grew nearer.

My plan, which I had discussed with Coach Hood at great length, was to gear my training to peak for the World Championships.

I would do so by staying in Abilene, getting my life back to a normal routine, forgetting about plane schedules and hotel reservations. It would be fun to spend some time with friends, play some golf, and maybe do a little water skiing.

Ironically, one of the most exciting things that has ever happened to me took place right in my hometown. I received a call from the mayor's office, advising me that plans were underway for a Billy Olson Day, complete with proclamations, the key to the city, and all the trimmings.

I've never before experienced the mixture of elation and discomfort that I felt at the ceremonies. I was well aware that there are any number of people in Abilene far more deserving of a special day than I am—men and women who have contributed greatly to the growth of the city, who have accomplished great things in the arts field, who have done far more than I have to direct the lives of youngsters in proper academic and spiritual paths. Thus it was a very humbling experience.

Still, there are few satisfactions as great as that of being recognized by the people to whom you are closest—neighbors, family, coaches, teachers. Officials from the City Council, Chamber of Commerce, Abilene High, and Abilene Christian were there. So were my parents and many of my former teammates. It was rewarding beyond words to realize I had such loyal support from my hometown.

And, to my surprise, the Jaycees announced the formation of a sponsorship fund to help me with living and training expenses as I prepared for my hoped-for participation in the Olympic Games. My mouth fell open when Pete Spano and Bill Orr, officials with the So-Tex Well Service and former pro football standouts, rose to announce that their company was getting the ball rolling with a donation of $10,000.

From time to time I get ribbed by some of my fellow athletes

about living in Abilene, Texas instead of Los Angeles or Dallas—
or one of the other major cities in the country. If they could have
been on hand for Billy Olson Day and felt the warmth and community involvement, I think the kidding would have ended rather
abruptly.

Few of them, I'm sure, will ever experience the same special
feeling I had that day.

In short order, I came to realize that the quiet pace of bygone
days was never going to return.

An advertising agency in Texas, having enjoyed a great deal of
success with world-champion diver Greg Louganis in a television
spot for Mercantile National Bank, called to ask if I would be
interested in doing a similar commercial.

The theme they used dealt with momentum. Frankly, the idea of
doing a commercial, something I'd thought was the sole property of
professional actors and maybe a pro football or baseball player
here and there, was exciting. So I was off to Los Angeles for three
days of filming a 30-second commercial.

After a great deal of standing around and about 30 vaults, they
finally had what they wanted.

I flew back to Texas more exhausted than I had ever felt returning from a track meet. What the director couldn't understand was
that vaulting over and over again at a height of 17 feet, 6 inches
can be taxing. And he repeatedly suggested that I could go through
my jumps at something less than full speed to conserve my energies. I was never fully able to convince him that it is impossible to
clear that height unless you approach the bar at full speed each
time! Otherwise, you're liable to wind up on your back on the
runway, waiting for the ambulance to arrive.

The Mercantile "momentum" commercial gave me more vis-
ibility than I ever dreamed it might. Shortly after it began running, people who didn't know me at all, who probably had never
been to a track meet in their lives, would come up and say, "Hey,
aren't you that momentum guy?" But I had to wonder about doing
something like that again.

When, in fact, a representative from the Adidas sports shoe
company called to ask if I was interested in doing a commercial for
them, I first asked how long it might take to do. They too wanted to

spend several days and have me vaulting a number of times each day. I told him of all the wasted time we had spent on the momentum commercial and suggested that we could get the footage they needed with only one day of vaulting. He said he would have to think about it and would get back to me. I never heard from him again.

Unless you're an athlete—a pole vaulter in particular—it is difficult to understand the strain the body endures when you vault time after time. The more tired you get, the more likely you are to injure yourself. And I was dead set on avoiding injuries at that point in my career.

Later, Dan Ripley agreed to do the commercial. Vaulting repeatedly during the two or three days that it took to film the commercial, he pulled a muscle and was sidelined for much of the 1983 season.

By the time the indoor season ended, I was aware of a new sensation, one I'd never experienced before in athletics. For the past several years I had been regarded as one of the top vaulters in the world, but still felt part of a group of a half-dozen or so who were capable of winning in major competition or bettering the world record if all was right. But as the 1983 outdoor season approached, I was suddenly the guy everyone else was shooting at.

It was a little like being the fast gun in the old Western movies—everyone wants to test you, to see if you're really as good as they've heard.

A columnist in one of the French papers talked with Thierry Vigneron and Pierre Quinon, two of the best vaulters in the world, and came to the conclusion that my 19-foot jump was nothing to be really concerned about since "Olson is strictly an indoor vaulter." Reading the clipping, which had been sent to a friend of mine, I wondered how they thought I had managed to be ranked number-one in the world outdoors the year before.

Then, voices from the past were being heard. Don Bragg, who had set the world record at 15 feet, 9¼ inches back in 1960, vaulting with a steel pole, began criticizing the fiberglass poles athletes use today. He said he would like to see how high I could go with the kind of pole he used. So certain was he that I would flop mightily, he said he was prepared to offer $10,000 to me or to anyone else who could clear 16 feet with a steel pole.

Steve Smith, who had been the first vaulter ever to clear 18 feet indoors, took a shot at it and couldn't get any higher than 15 feet. I saw no reason to try it. I had enough on my hands, learning to use the fiberglass pole.

With the outdoor season already underway, I continued to hold back, turning down invitations to early meets in favor of lifting weights and working on my technique. But I was getting eager for a return to competition. My growing impatience was, I felt, a good sign. The weariness of the indoor campaign was gone.

In late March, Earl Bell came to Abilene to vault in a meet Coach Hood was having at Abilene Christian. I cleared 18 feet, 8¼ inches and had a couple of good tries at 19-1.

It was time to get back on the road.

James Blackwood, the assistant track coach at the University of Texas, has followed Billy Olson's career since he first began vaulting. A standout half-miler and captain of the Abilene High track team before accepting a scholarship to Abilene Christian, Blackwood admits he made a mistake not offering Billy a full scholarship to attend Texas.

"Back then," he says, "what you had to consider was how productive an athlete could be in meets where you were fighting for the team championship. Our full scholarships went to guys who could pick up points in a variety of events.

"Still, if we had had any idea Billy was going to be as good as he's become. . . ."

Olson holds no grudges. Today, in fact, he's close friends with Blackwood.

"A week or so before the Texas Relays," Blackwood recalls, "I called Billy to ask if he would come to the meet. I knew of his plans to take it a little slower in the early part of the outdoor season, but I also knew he enjoyed jumping in Austin.

"When I called he seemed a bit hesitant. It was one of those 'Well, maybe' kind of conversations. I was a little puzzled."

Blackwood's initial impression was that Billy had joined ranks

with the many top track-and-field athletes who hold out for an
"appearance fee" before agreeing to compete in certain major meets.
The fees, which range from a few hundred to several thousand
dollars, are generally paid under the table.

It is a practice in which University of Texas head coach Cleburne
Price, who also serves as the Texas Relays meet director, has stub-
bornly refused to participate.

A bit puzzled by Olson's hesitancy, Blackwood pursued the mat-
ter. "Is it going to take something more than travel expenses to get
you here?" Blackwood finally asked.

"That's about the size of it," Billy replied.

The seconds of silence that followed were an indication of Black-
wood's surprise.

Finally, he asked, "What's it going to take?"

Now Billy was laughing, clearly enjoying the put-on. "If I come
down there," he told his old friend, "you're going to have to play golf
with me after church Sunday. And we've got to be finished early
because I've promised to speak to a youth group there that evening."

"You're on," Blackwood said.

In the warm sunshine of Austin I cleared 18-8¼, got a good case
of sunburn, and beat Blackwood on the eighteenth hole. All in all,
it was a good weekend.

I returned home fully convinced that I was ready to have an
outstanding outdoor season.

Two days later, the bottom fell out.

Running 100-yard sprints on the Abilene Christian track, I was
running at top speed when a distance runner stepped onto the
track directly in front of me. I saw him but didn't slow down,
assuming he would step out of the way. Instead, for some unknown
reason, he froze. Just before I would have collided with him, I side-
stepped at full speed—and felt a hot pain shoot through the muscles in my hip.

Even before I could stop I knew I had pulled a muscle.

Within a matter of days I realized it was serious. There simply
was no way I could run without considerable pain. The only thing
to do was stay off the track for a while. Rest and treatment, I hoped,
would resolve the problem in a couple of weeks.

The fact that I was going to lose valuable training time, not to mention competition, frustrated me a great deal. Patience, as I have mentioned before, is not one of my shining virtues.

After a month of doing very little, I decided to test the hip. Vigneron and his fellow Frenchman Patrick Abada had indicated they would participate in the California Relays and, anxious to prove to them that I was something more than a good indoor vaulter, I decided to compete there, too.

Despite the fact that I had not vaulted at all for a month, I felt I could do well. Technically, I might be a bit rusty, but I was still in excellent shape.

One of the problems I've dealt with throughout my athletic career is the fact that my mind has often gotten ahead of my physical capabilities. I think I can do things my body isn't prepared to do. The trip to California was a prime example.

I took one vault and reinjured the hip.

Looking back, I can see I was probably two weeks away from being fully healed and ready to return to training. But I had pushed things and would have to suffer for it.

For the first time since breaking my wrist, I allowed myself to wallow in self-pity. Unable to compete, I felt virtually useless. Instead of going out to the track each day to lift weights, I stayed away. Staying around the house, doing nothing, I lost weight.

Despite encouragement from Coach Hood and Brad Pursley, I couldn't seem to muster any motivation. The big plans I had laid for the season were ruined. Finally, I went to Coach Hood to see what he thought about my just calling it a year. I was ready to store my poles and get as far away from the sport as I could until the next season. For the first time in my life, I was tired of pole vaulting.

Coach Hood would have none of it. It was, he pointed out, a long time until the World Championships in Helsinki. If I took my time getting well and could manage to vault well enough at the national championships to earn one of the three vault spots on the United States team, I just might be back in shape in time to achieve the goal I had set for the season. Or, at least, one of my goals. The world record, I knew, would have to wait. But maybe the world championship was still possible.

With my enthusiasm at something less than full steam, I slowly began to convince myself that the season could be salvaged. But I felt as if I was in slow motion while the rest of the world was doing double time.

Pursley, improving by leaps and bounds, established a new American outdoor record when he cleared 18-10¼. Then, just weeks later, Jeff Buckingham, who had vaulted well during the previous indoor season, broke Brad's record by a half-inch. Word from Europe was that the Soviet Union vaulters and the French were doing well.

And Billy Olson was jogging around the track a couple of days a week, wondering if he was ever going to be able to run at full speed again.

By mid-June I was ready to have another try at it. The national championships were scheduled to be held in Indianapolis. There the U.S. team which would travel to Helsinki in August would be chosen.

My frame of mind was dramatically different from that I had enjoyed as I traveled to the nationals the year before. Then I had won and established a new meet record. This time I wasn't sure what to expect. I felt certain the injury was completely healed, but the amount of training I had lost concerned me. I wasn't at all sure I had either the strength or the speed to do what I hoped to do.

At Indianapolis I had one good jump. At 18 feet, 1½ inches, Buckingham cleared on his first attempt. I got over on my third try.

Neither of us was able to get over 18-4, and the meet was over. Jeff was awarded first place on fewer misses, and I was second. For the first time in a long time, I didn't feel really disappointed with second. I had made the World Championships team and had felt no pain in my hip during the competition.

Still, I wasn't running well and knew that, until I was, I couldn't expect to vault really well. I told meet officials that I would bypass the U.S.-East Germany dual meet scheduled for the following weekend in Los Angeles and would just concentrate on getting ready for Helsinki.

I was convinced I would be unbeatable by August.

My plan was to go to Europe and participate in a series of six meets there before the World Championships. By doing so, I could reacquaint myself with the conditions that you can always expect abroad. Most meets there are held in large stadiums built for soccer, and you can almost always bet on there being a crazy, swirling wind to battle against. Strength is far more important to a vaulter in those conditions than the ones generally faced in the United States.

Unfortunately, strength was something of which I was in short supply. Too many workouts had been missed, too much idle time had passed while I waited for my injury to heal. My European plan was stupid.

In London, Nice, and Luxembourg I failed to clear a single height. Whatever confidence I had was gone. I contacted directors of the other meets in which I was to participate and advised them I was returning to the United States.

Though I was frustrated and depressed, the fact that there was still a month remaining before the World Championships gave me hope. Coach Hood outlined a program of weight lifting, running, and gymnastics that he felt would get me ready to compete well in Helsinki.

At some informal summer meets held at ACU, I vaulted well again, clearing 18-6. My chances, I decided, had improved to about 50-50. Maybe I could be a factor in the competition. But in order for me to win, everything would have to go perfectly.

Suffice it to say I didn't receive a hero's welcome when I checked into the U.S. team headquarters at Helsinki. In fact, I arrived in a rather bad mood, looking for one of the team officials named Berny Wagner.

A few days before I was to leave the States, I had received a call from high-jumper Dwight Stones, telling me I was deep in the doghouse. There had been an international meet in Stockholm two weeks before the World Championships in which most of the U.S. athletes were to participate. Evidently, Wagner, an official with The Athletics Congress, had assured meet directors that everyone would be on hand.

Just about everyone was. After all, the majority of the American athletes had been in Europe for weeks, competing. I was one of the few team members still in the States.

Stones told me Wagner was furious that none of the U.S. pole vaulters had competed. Buckingham hadn't made it; neither had Mike Tully, the third member of the U.S. pole-vault delegation, who had been touring Europe all summer. Neither, for that matter, had sprinter and long jumper Carl Lewis.

"They're looking for someone to use as an example," Stones said, "and all indications are you've drawn the black bean simply because you aren't over here. I don't see how they can take you off the team since you earned your spot, but I just thought you ought to know what's going on."

It was the World Cup all over again. Furious, I began making calls. Finally, I reached John Jackson, one of the TAC officials who wasn't in Europe. He said he had heard nothing about my being replaced on the team and assured me all would be settled by the time I reached Helsinki.

At that point, I felt the trip would be worth it just to confront Wagner.

When we finally did meet, the scene wasn't one of those you look back on with great amounts of pride. A full-scale shouting match erupted almost immediately. I told him it was foolish for him to have expected me to travel all the way from Abilene to Stockholm to compete in a meet that was of no real importance. It was, it seemed to me, far more important to prepare as best I could for the World Championships.

Wagner was clearly in no mood to reason. Yes, he admitted, he had been trying to get me replaced on the team. "And why not?" he said. "If you get right down to it, you've never really done anything other than your indoor world record."

I was livid. I asked if he had bothered to check the world outdoor rankings the year before. "That was me in the number-one spot, remember? I can't believe you're trying to do this. It doesn't make sense."

And it doesn't to this day. I find it hard to believe that my absence at that one track meet is the only reason for Berny Wagner's attitude toward me. But I have no idea what else it might be. Chances are I won't ever find out, since he and I have made sure we give each other considerable room anytime we're at the same meet.

To further complicate matters, I found out that Stan Huntsman, the U.S. coach, had sided with Wagner in an attempt to have me replaced on the team.

Welcome to the United States track-and-field team, Billy. And best of luck.

Things went downhill from there.

Despite the unsettling sequence of events, I was looking forward to participating in the meet. For the first time in track-and-field history, there would be a recognized world championship meet, and it was exciting to be involved in such a historic event.

The stadium would be the same which had been used for the 1952 Olympic Games, and it was familiar to me. In fact, I had set the stadium record there two years earlier, clearing 18 feet, 2½ inches.

By the time the competition was to get underway, I had put all other thoughts aside and was ready to concentrate on nothing but vaulting.

Mother Nature, however, made that difficult.

On the day the pole-vault preliminaries were to be held, a forecast of rain kept worried officials and competitors glancing skyward. Heavy, rumbling clouds hung over the stadium, and a chilling wind was blowing.

I had decided I would wait until the bar reached 17 feet, 8 inches before entering the competition. By that time, however, rain was falling so hard you couldn't see the pit from the end of the runway.

As the vaulters sat under a covered area, watching the rain form puddles throughout the stadium, my enthusiasm bottomed out. I knew I had absolutely no chance of performing well under those conditions, and I suspect most of the other vaulters were feeling the same way.

Still, the meet officials held out, hoping the weather might clear. After an hour, they announced that the vault was canceled and that we would start over the next morning.

That created even more controversy within the ranks. Since I hadn't even attempted a vault, I would, in effect, be fresh the following day while the others had expended energies on several jumps. I sensed that several of the vaulters were upset with me— that they felt I had gained an unfair advantage.

On the other hand, I heard no criticism of the fact that several vaulters had missed their three attempts and had been eliminated, even though, with the officials' ruling, they were to be allowed to return to the competition.

There was a great deal of tension in the air and it disturbed me. I've always looked at competition as a friendly pursuit. And I doubt there is a group of athletes in any sport as close as pole vaulters. Oh, there are going to be times when you get upset with someone— that's a natural part of competition—but I've never held a grudge against anyone who beat me. Nor have I ever felt that anyone has begrudged my wins. I've always felt that if you were friends going into the competition, there was no reason not to be friends during and after.

In Helsinki, however, there were suddenly a lot of unfriendly faces.

The following day the preliminaries were scheduled to begin early in the morning. But when we reported to the track it was misting rain and winter cold. All the vaulters gathered in a meeting room before the officials arrived and Mike Tully took charge.

"There's no way any of us can hope to perform well in these conditions," he told the gathering, "so we've got to stick together. What we've got to do is tell the officials we aren't going to vault until the weather is suitable. If we all stick together, there's nothing they can do but agree. If we're divided, however, they'll use that against us and make us vault."

It was funny. Mike was up there, sounding like a Teamsters man, forming what has to be the first pole-vaulters union in the history of the sport. I admired his powers of persuasion. When he finished, a vote was taken, and all but a couple of the vaulters agreed to stand their ground.

Fortunately, however, the situation never developed to a point where we would have to refuse to compete. One of the officials came into the room and informed us that a decision had been made to pass every vaulter on hand to the finals.

Thus we all returned to our rooms for another day of waiting.

On the third day I awoke to find it still raining. Worse, I had lost my edge. Enthusiastic and confident the first two days of the aborted competition, my spirits were beginning to sag. I had come to Helsinki realizing that I was not in ideal physical shape. But my mental attitude had been good. Now, I wasn't sure I had that going for me either.

By the time the competition got underway, I knew.

At breakfast I saw one of the U.S. trainers and asked if he would meet me at the stadium early to do some work on my back. He said sure, and we agreed on a time. For whatever reason, he never showed up.

Seeing personal doctors accompanying each of the Soviet athletes and realizing that I wasn't even going to be able to get a rubdown before the competition irritated me further.

The day had all the marks of a really bad experience.

If anything, the conditions were worse than they had been on the day the vault competition was supposed to have begun. There was little rain, but the temperatures were in the 40s, and a 15-to-20-mile-per-hour wind was blowing in the faces of the vaulters.

Occasionally, however, there would be a calm. Thus most of the vaulters waited at the top of the runway, their two-minute time allotment for a vault ticking away, hoping the wind would die down before they ran out of time.

To complicate matters, it was difficult to tell what the wind was doing in the area of the pit. Because it was swirling so, it might appear to be still at the top of the runway where the vaulter was standing but be blowing crazily near the pit.

Before the competition got underway, Buckingham, Tully, and I got together and worked out a system. Since international rules forbid any manner of coaching during competition, you are not allowed help of any kind, even from fellow competitors.

What we agreed on was a system whereby two of us would stand near the pit while the other was vaulting. If, for instance, Tully and I looked straight at Buckingham as he prepared for his run, it would indicate the wind was bad and for him not to begin. If we looked away, that would be his sign to have at it.

When I got up for my first vault, Jeff and Mike did nothing but stare directly at me. Actually, they didn't need to because it was obvious to me that the wind conditions were terrible.

Vladimir Polyakov of the Soviet Union, the first 19-foot vaulter in history, was just ahead of me in the order and had been blown so far to one side as he went up into his vault that he missed the pit.

With 20 seconds left on the time clock, I decided to make my first attempt at 17 feet, 8½ inches. Five steps into my run, a gust of wind blew me completely off the runway. So much for the first attempt.

My second try wasn't much better. With the wind still gusting and my teammates giving the signal for me to wait, I made up my mind that I was going to plant the pole regardless. I did, but never even made it up to the bar.

I did everything I knew to prepare myself mentally for the final vault. But to no avail. I made an embarrassing attempt, knocked the bar off, and was out of the competition without so much as clearing the opening height.

Buckingham did manage to clear the opening height, and earned the best American finish—thirteenth.

A powerful Soviet teenager named Sergei Bubka was outstanding, finally clearing 18 feet, 8¼ inches to win the gold medal. Konstantin Volkov, also of the U.S.S.R., was second at 18-4½.

Disappointed and embarrassed, all I could think of was getting away from Helsinki and back home as quickly as possible. I had made a commitment to compete in a meet in Italy the week after the World Championships and, thinking it would be foolish for me to prolong what had already been an agonizing season, I spent most of the night on the phone trying to get out of any further competitions. That finally accomplished, I went to work on arranging a flight back to the U.S.

Flying home, weary and upset over the way things had gone in recent months, I tried to think through all that had happened. In a year's time I had gone from being the number-one-ranked vaulter in the world to failing to make the opening height at the biggest meet of the year.

Even in my black mood, however, I was already regretting some of the jesting remarks I had made to reporters after the competition. I had suggested that maybe the wear and tear of competition had become more than I wanted to continue. I hadn't come right out and said it, but they had gone away with the impression, I think, that I was considering calling it quits.

I knew that wasn't going to happen. Not with the Olympic Games just around the corner. I was discouraged and more than a little frustrated, but I don't think I ever got to the point where I doubted my abilities as an athlete.

On the other hand, I realized it would be necessary to reestablish myself. In the days to come I would hear that I was a "choker" who couldn't perform well in the big meets. And there would be those who echoed the opinion of Berny Wagner—that I was strictly an "indoor vaulter" who couldn't deal with the outside, where it rained and got cold and the wind blew.

For most participants, the first World Track and Field Championships had been a great experience. And American athletes had performed well. Mary Decker, facing the challenge of the Soviet distance runners, had been a double winner in the 1,500- and 3,000-meter runs. Carl Lewis had been magnificent as he won the 100 meters and the long jump, then anchored the United States four-by-100-meter relay to a new world record.

Back home, millions had cheered their performance on television. Newspapers had celebrated their achievements with banner headlines.

The reviews of the pole vault, however, had been less than glowing. In the *Chicago Tribune,* writer Don Pierson had called my effort "a pathetic show." Another newspaper had said the U.S. vaulters were the biggest flop of the meet. Not the kind of thing you like to clip for your scrapbook.

I kept them, however. At this very moment they are tucked away in my billfold—constant reminders.

Back home, I made up my mind to forget about the season, about pole vaulting, for a while. I would relax, then sit down with Coach Hood and determine the best plan of attack for the 1984 season.

It wasn't easy, however, to ignore the fact that for many the season was still going on. And that others were improving while I sat doing nothing.

In Cologne, just weeks after the World Championships, France's Pierre Quinon jumped into the headlines. Like me, he had failed to clear a height in Helsinki, but had come back with a world-record clearance of 19 feet, 1 inch.

Three days later, in Rome, his fellow countryman, Thierry Vigneron, who had done no better than eighth at the World Championships, bettered Quinon's record by clearing 19 feet, 1½ inches.

Suddenly, it seemed, the sky was getting crowded with vaulters clearing 19 feet.

9

The Olympic Season

THERE IS, *in this business of serving as a literary Boswell to another, the rare reward of getting to know someone on a fairly intimate basis in a relatively short period of time. The working arrangement necessary to do a book like the one now in your hands is such that it provides the interviewer something of a carte blanche entré into personal matters a casual acquaintance would never dare suggest as topics of conversation.*

It is a task which also offers galloping frustrations and teeth-grinding pitfalls. Billy Olson, quite frankly, can be modest to a fault when it comes to discussion of things other than his athletic accomplishments. Keep the conversation steered toward his pole vaulting and he will, without so much as a blink of the eye, tell you confidently that he regards himself as one of the best. Which is to say false modesty is not a shortcoming he can be accused of. But he is also a very private kind of young man despite the easy, outgoing nature which has made him a favorite of magazine writers, track fans, and friends from hither to yon. And so there were times, during the preparation of his story, when either his memory was remarkably poor or he simply saw no need to dwell on matters he deemed unimportant to the advancement of the story line.

For that reason, I often did literary end runs—with his approval— to learn more about the private side. To properly get to know the Billy Olson who retreats from the spotlight of the athletic arena, I decided, takes more time than an impatient publisher's deadline allows.

For instance, it was Coach Hood, not Billy, who first told me of the numerous requests that arrive from coaches, families, and just-beginning vaulters in need of tips or an encouraging word.

"Not long ago," Hood said, "Billy got a call from a junior-high coach who had a promising young pole vaulter whose mother had been killed in an automobile accident. The boy was devastated and had, for all practical purposes, given up on life. He had quit the track team, his grades had fallen off drastically, and socially he had retreated into a shell. No one—not the local minister, friends of the family, or concerned classmates—had been able to bring the youngster out of his depression."

Maybe, the coach suggested, a word from Billy, whom the troubled teenager greatly admired, might help.

"Billy was really concerned about the situation," Hood continued, "and he came to me to ask what I thought he should say. He wanted to help if he could, but he was concerned that he might say the wrong thing. We sat in my office and talked about it for some time. I told him just to be honest with the boy, to talk with him and then see if there was something he might do that would help. Quite frankly, I didn't know what to tell him."

Thus Hood left it at that.

He had, in fact, forgotten about the matter by the time a letter arrived a few weeks later, addressed to him. It came from the troubled youngster's coach. He was writing, he said, to let him know what Billy had done.

"I'm sure he contacted Billy as well," Hood said, "but Billy never mentioned it to me. Evidently, he had gotten in touch with the youngster and had pointed out that he was certain his mother would not have wanted him to give up, that she would have been greatly saddened if he chose not to pursue those things for which he obviously had a talent."

Encouraged by Billy Olson's concern for his personal problems, the young man returned to vaulting. At last report he had established a new school record and was again high on the list of honor-roll students.

In the mind of Billy Olson, such matters are not grist for the literary wheel; they are private and no cause for personal breast-beating. It is part of his Christian philosophy that good deeds are worth far more when done in private.

"Yeah, I remember that," he would say when confronted with such an anecdote. "You know, the thing that comes to mind when I think about that kid is that he helped me more than I did him. Here was a guy who felt really alone, who was certain that the only person who had really cared about him was gone. I've never had that feeling. All my life I've had more people than I can count who were standing right there to encourage me, support me, and give me whatever kind of help I needed. You just don't stop and think about things like that very often. That kid made me take stock."

Which was what I was doing as I drove toward Abilene one early January morning. The book was nearing completion and a new indoor season was underway—proving, I suppose, that any kind of history is never really completed.

In the next couple of days, I knew, I would ask the last professional questions necessary to complete the manuscript. From that point, my relationship with the young man I had come to admire greatly would take a more informal turn.

With only the mindless banter of a couple of early-morning disc jockeys as company, I drove through the sparse openness of West Texas, reflecting on the manner in which the story would reach its end. I smiled as I recalled Billy's remarks following his return from Helsinki. "Don't," he had said, "end the book there."

I promised him that would not be the case. In exchange, I persuaded him to allow me to assume the narrative in this, the final chapter.

Though he would never admit it, I think he privately wished the book could be kept from the publisher until after the upcoming Olympic Games. Los Angeles, with its possibilities of a storybook ending, a possible gold medal, would close things out with drums beating and bugles blaring.

The Olympic Games, of course, are constantly on his mind, and there was seldom a conversation when they did not come up in some manner. Still, I had come to realize, they are not the end-all to the Billy Olson story.

How, I wondered, would he take it if he did not realize his goal of winning the gold medal? In a society which only salutes champions and immediately forgets the name of the athlete who finished second, would he pass undue stern judgment on himself?

"I've gone over that in my mind a million times," he said. "The Olympic Games are very important to me, and I'm putting a great deal of emphasis on them. But I'm trying to be realistic. I don't want to go to Los Angeles and lose in the Olympic Games and have that taint the memories of the good things that have happened to me in sports.

"I've had a good career, I've set some records, and I'm very proud of what I've accomplished. But yes, I dearly want that gold medal."

It is perhaps proper for me to admit here that I, too, want him to have it.

Not because an Olympic championship might make his book more attractive in the marketplace (though I don't guard my amateur status nearly as passionately as does Billy), but because, as an unabashed admirer, I want to see him enjoy that final success.

Having spent a great deal of my adult life chronicling the victories and defeats of athletes, I have come to realize how effective well-known sports figures can be as role models. I will not judge whether it is right or wrong, but the truth remains that a standout performance in the athletic arena seems to stir more national emotion than a moon landing multiplied by a Nobel Prize-winning breakthrough in science.

In an age of too many stories of athletes battling drug abuse, flaunting monster egos and balking at megabuck contracts, Billy Olson is a breath of fresh air. Sports needs more ambassadors like him.

Such were my thoughts as I drove. I was also thinking of the events that had transpired in Billy's life since we last had sat and talked.

The disappointment of Helsinki had dulled and the injury which had turned his most recent outdoor season into a week-after-week frustration was fully healed.

The year 1983 was behind him and a new season, an Olympic year, awaited.

After long talks with his coach, Billy had mapped a plan which, he said, would take him to a peak during the Olympic summer. He would compete in ten or so indoor meets, then rest for a couple of months before getting back to competition outdoors. In the past, he admitted, he had ended the grueling indoor campaign weary and gone directly to outdoor competition without proper time for rest and training. This time, he insisted, things would be different.

Over the phone he outlined his indoor schedule to me: He would open the season with back-to-back meets in Canada, then go on to Los Angeles, Johnson City, New York, Dallas, and—oh, by the way—he had been invited to participate in the ABC-TV-sponsored Superstars competition.

There was an electric enthusiasm in his voice. I hung up the phone certain that new celestial heights were just around the corner.

The morning after he was to have competed in Ottawa, my first waking thought was to collect the paper from the front yard and see how well he had performed. A small item on the meet, buried on one of the back pages of the sports section, told of his attempting 18-1 three times and missing on each. In the vernacular of pole vaulting, he had no-heighted.

The winner, 1980 Olympic champion Wladyslaw Kozakiewicz of Poland, had opened at 17-9 and claimed the gold medal by default. Earl Bell, Brad Pursley, and another Polish vaulter, Tadeusz Slusarski, had all failed to clear a height.

For Billy, the second night was no better. In Sherbrooke, Quebec, he failed to clear 18 feet, ½ inch.

My weekend was spent in a blue funk. I fiddled at the typewriter, not producing a readable word. Was Billy injured? Maybe he was not yet conditioned as well as he had led me to believe. Perhaps his plan for the new season was to start more slowly than before. But, if so, why compete when he wasn't ready? Was he feeling new pressures of which I was unaware?

For a couple of days I fought the urge to give him a call, to see if all was well. Instead, I decided to wait. We had already made plans to get together a couple of weeks later, so I had no real justification for seeking him out. I decided to keep my nose to the grindstone and out of his business.

The following week things went better. At the Sunkist Invitational in Los Angeles, Billy managed his first win of the season, clearing 18 feet, 8¼ inches. Among those he defeated was France's Pierre Quinon, who had briefly held the outdoor record at 19 feet, ¼

inch the summer before. Billy had faced his first real challenger for
the Olympic gold medal and won.

But then, the following night in Johnson City, Tennessee, Jeff
Buckingham established a new record at the Eastman Invitational,
clearing 18-6½. Olson was second with 18 feet, ½ inch.

I called Coach Hood. "He's vaulting very well," he said in a com-
forting tone. "No real problems. He's been experimenting with a new
pole, though, and it's taking some getting used to. But he's confident. He'll be going very high before the indoor season is over. In
fact, I wouldn't be surprised to see him set a world record before too
long."

To do so, however, he would have to go considerably beyond the
mark he had set in Toronto a year earlier. Sergei Bubka, the Soviet
vaulter who had emerged as the surprise winner in Helsinki, was
fast making it clear he should not be judged a fluke.

In an indoor meet in Moscow, Bubka had competed against vaulters from Hungary and Bulgaria and had added a quarter of an inch
to Billy's existing record. Two weeks later, in an international meet
in Milan, Italy, Bubka had improved on the record again, vaulting
19 feet, ¾ of an inch. At age 20, he had become only the second man
ever to clear 19 feet indoors.

Clearly, Billy had a new challenger to contend with.

And word was that Bubka and teammate Konstantin Volkov
were planning a trip to the United States. Before the indoor season
was over, then, Billy would get a chance to test himself against the
vaulters which Track & Field News had ranked one and two in the
world at the end of the '83 season.

First, however, Olson had to deal with one of those weekend
schedules only the young would even contemplate. The ABC Superstars event, matching a variety of standout athletes from different
sports, had sounded like fun. Practicing for such events as tennis,
bowling, and golf would provide a welcome diversion from pole
vaulting.

When Billy agreed to join the likes of Los Angeles Raiders football
standouts Marcus Allen and Cliff Branch, lightweight boxing
champion Ray (Boom Boom) Mancini and fellow track athletes
Greg Foster and Tom Petranoff in the weekend competition, it is

unlikely that he realized the logistic difficulties he would be forced to deal with.

On Friday night he was in New York to compete in the annual Millrose Games in Madison Square Garden. Despite allergy problems which had made the Dallas-to-New York flight a painful experience, he won with a height of 18 feet, 8¼ inches.

Then, after midnight, he and Greg Foster, winner of the 60-yard high hurdles, boarded a red-eye flight to Florida.

At nine the next morning he was on the tennis court at Key Biscayne, participating in the first of seven events on the two-day Superstars program. Suffice it to say he didn't fare too well on opening day.

The spotlight, in fact, had shone on Petranoff, the world-record holder in the javelin throw. One of the lesser knowns in the field of Super Bowl heroes and pro boxers, Petranoff had demolished the competition in the first day, assuring himself of the overall title even if he didn't get out of bed on Sunday.

The battle, then, was for second place as the second round of competition got underway.

Rested, Billy fared much better. In the 100-yard dash, he lost by a whisker to Raiders wide receiver Branch, once a world-class sprinter himself, as both were timed in 9.6. He finished second to Petranoff in the swimming event and was third in the half-mile run, which Foster won easily.

Then came the final event of the competition—the obstacle course, an event which requires the participants to scale a wall, get through a tunnel, run through a maze of tires, push a blocking sled, long jump over a water obstacle, high jump, then finish with a series of hurdles. It is the kind of event only the minds of television could design. Billy was third, finishing behind Petranoff and Foster.

When all was said and done, it was the sport of track and field which emerged as the winner of the whole competition. Petranoff had accumulated a total of 61 points, a new Superstars record, to claim the title. Foster was second with 35½ points, and Billy placed third with 27.

"Greg kept giving me a hard time all through the competition," Billy remembers. "He kept telling me if I hadn't been sleepwalking all through the first day of events I might have done better. He

reminded me that he had dealt with the same lack of sleep and done pretty well.

"I pointed out that it had taken him all of seven seconds to win the hurdles in New York. The pole vault competition had lasted four hours."

It had been that kind of competition—good-natured, fun, full of barbs and jibes tossed among the talented collection of athletes on hand.

But enough was enough. Billy, more tired than he'd been in weeks, was anxious to get back to Abilene, to rest, and to get back to the more serious business of pole vaulting.

As he waited in the airport for his flight to be called, he picked up a paper and read an account of the pole vault at the Horizon Invitational in Chicago, a meet he had decided to bypass to keep his Superstars commitment.

Earl Bell, who had been second at the Millrose Games on Friday, had cleared 18-1½ on his first attempt, then decided not to try to go higher because he had not brought the pole he felt necessary to attempt a record. Jeff Buckingham, meanwhile, had passed to 19 feet, 1 inch and made two impressive tries at the height.

"At the top of the bar," he had told reporters, "I dropped my chest. If I had stayed concave over the bar I would have had the world record."

A week later, Billy knew, he would face Buckingham, Bell, and Pierre Quinon in the Dallas Times Herald *Invitational.*

Obviously, things weren't going to get any easier.

As indoor track-and-field meets go, the Dallas Times-Herald Invitational *(sponsored by a local newspaper which got the brainstorm from its corporate big brother, the* Los Angeles Times*) is a new kid on the block. In New York, for instance, they first started holding indoor meets in the late 1860s in the old Empire Skating Rink, laying a board track down over the ice. In time, competition would move to the old Madison Square Garden, then to the new Madison Square Garden, and finally out to the Meadowlands over in East Rutherford, New Jersey. And always the fans followed, enthusiastic and knowledgeable.*

But in Dallas, where football is king and the Dallas Cowboys are credited with everything from winning Super Bowls to pulling a dispirited community from the post-Kennedy-assassination doldrums, track and field was an athletic stepchild. A sports information director for a Texas university with a longstanding reputation for fielding great football teams once voiced the general feeling the public held for the sport: "The only thing more boring than track," he said, "is field."

A man named Ted McLaughlin began changing all that a few years ago. The track coach at Southern Methodist, he was placed in charge of organizing the Times-Herald meet and set about to bring in the finest talent in the sport. World and American records fell the first time the meet was held. Athletes applauded the manner in which the meet was run, the condition of the track, and the enthusiasm of those fans who turned out to the Reunion Arena event.

Among those who professed a special feeling for the Dallas meet was Billy Olson. Just a three-hour drive from Abilene, the Times-Herald competition was a meet where his family and friends could come to see him perform. The 1984 meet was to be no exception.

All week, members of the media quizzed him about the possibility of a world record. But Billy, remembering that every time he had predicted such a feat he had not performed well, resisted the urge.

Privately, he hoped the time might be right. There would be no meet on Friday to tax his strength. He would go to Dallas fresh. The competition would be excellent and the crowd, he knew, would give him a lift.

In recent years, it had become almost a tradition to disregard everything else going on in the three-ring-circus atmosphere of an indoor meet when Olson walked to the top of the runway. It was obvious he was a crowd favorite.

Sitting in the stands, my wife marveled at the enthusiasm the sellout crowd demonstrated for Billy. "They love him," she said more than once, "and he seems to return that feeling. He's out there having a good time, and it seems to infect everyone in the place."

Indeed, few athletes now competing play to a crowd in the way Olson can. There is nothing arrogant or show-off about his approach, but he encourages those on hand to help him in his efforts. When applause begins, a wide smile breaks across his face and he *acknowledges it—and in doing so brings on another wave of clapping and cheering.*

Then, each successful jump is followed by a celebration: Billy clapping, raising his arms over his head, smiling—always smiling. If he misses, there is a gesture of apology and the hint of promise to do better on the next attempt.

Suffice it to say Billy Olson is one of the major reasons for the success of the meet. "If we had a contest to select the most popular athlete at the meet each year," says meet director McLaughlin, "Billy would have already retired the trophy."

It would be the first time I had seen Billy vault indoors all season. And, like the 15,000 others on hand, I wondered if perhaps it might be a night when a new world record would be set.

It was not, however, a question I posed to Billy as we chatted before the competition. Rather, we talked about the Superstars competition, which he had appeared to survive in good fashion and reaffirmed our meeting a few days hence in Abilene.

That done, I faded into the background to watch as he prepared for the competition at hand. It never fails to amaze me how casual the great athletes appear even as their moments of truth approach. While several other vaulters were already in the process of warming up, testing poles, marking the runway to be certain their steps were right, Billy looked, for all practical purposes, like a spectator. He talked with friends in the stands, visited with fellow athletes who stopped by to say hello and wish him luck, signed autographs, and smiled a great deal.

If a world record was on his mind, I could not discern the fact.

The other vaulters, it seemed to me, were more intense, more grim-faced as they went about their preparation. Quinon, a handsome young Frenchman with little knowledge of the English language, kept to himself most of the time, speaking only to fellow countryman Patrick Abada, who had accompanied him on his trip to the United States.

And Jeff Buckingham looked less like a world-class athlete than anyone I'd ever seen. Short and stocky, he wore his hair shoulder length and had a full beard. Standing near Frank Estes, who had driven up from Odessa to see his former college roommate vault, I mentioned my surprise at the physical appearance of Buckingham.

*Frank only shook his head. "That's Jeff Buckingham?" he mar-
veled. I was pleased my reaction wasn't that off-base.*

*Earl Bell, accompanied by his wife, who carried a movie camera
with which she would take films of her husband and the other
competitors (films Earl would later study at great length), was the
elder statesman of the group. A warm, polite young man of 28, he
smiled often as well-wishers spoke. But no sooner would they go
back to their seats than his face would take on a serious look.*

*Before beginning his preparations, he spoke with his wife in the
stands, evidently giving her instructions on what to film.*

*It was ironic, I thought. No doubt she would be filming the vaults
Billy would make. And at some later time, in his home back in
Arkansas, Earl Bell would study the form of his friend and rival,
looking for some technique only the trained eye could isolate—something that might help him in his own bid to claim the world record
and the Olympic gold medal.*

*Billy chose to wait and enter the competition only after the bar
had been raised to 18 feet, 4¼ inches, a height Quinon, Bell, and
Buckingham had cleared.*

*Twice he appeared to have cleared the bar, only to knock it off as
he fell toward the pit. Suddenly he was but one vault away from
elimination, from no-heighting as he had done weeks earlier in
Canada.*

*But on his third attempt he powered down the wooden runway,
his feet seeming barely to touch the surface as he ran. There was the
pole plant and the sudden jerk that catapulted him in the direction
of the arena's ceiling. In a split second he was over cleanly, clearing
the bar by what seemed to be almost a foot.*

*The bar went to 18 feet, 8¾ inches. Buckingham missed three
times and was out. Bell, feeling a slight twinge in his leg, decided
not to vault at the height, leaving the battle to Olson and the standout Frenchman.*

*On his first attempt Billy was over, erasing his own meet record.
Quinon made it on his third attempt.*

*The two vaulters talked with meet officials and decided to have
the bar raised to 19-1. The public address announcer advised those*

on hand that the vaulters were attempting a new indoor world-record height.

Neither really came close, and Billy was awarded first place on fewer misses. He had now faced Quinon three times and won all three. That and the fact that he had cleared 18 feet, 8¾ inches three weeks in a row—a sign that his consistency had returned—pleased him.

But, speaking with reporters in the interview area afterward, he admitted he was disappointed that the record had not come on that night. "I felt so good tonight," he said. "I felt I had clouds under my feet. Everything seemed perfect. I thought I vaulted well, but I'm disappointed. The record has to come. That's all there is to it."

With that he was off—to seek out those who had come to cheer him on, to sign more autographs, and to thank those who had driven from Abilene to watch him compete.

By the time he was ready to leave, the meet had long been over and workmen were beginning to tear down the track and replace the basketball court for an NBA game scheduled for the next afternoon.

As he walked from the building into the crisp night air, surrounded by youngsters holding up programs for him to sign, Billy stopped and snapped his fingers. "I forgot to pick up my medal," he said. Then he continued walking.

For Billy Olson, it occurred to me, medals and trophies were no longer the important things.

The purpose of my trip to Abilene two days later was not just to prime Billy's recollection of past triumphs and amusing stories. I especially wanted to spend a couple of days observing the routine an athlete preparing for an Olympic bid goes through.

What I would learn is that getting ready for the Olympics is a full-time pursuit, light years removed from the quieter, more casual approach of collegiate athletics.

Monday morning I sat listening as Billy talked long distance to a vaulting-pole manufacturer about a specific design he had in mind. He spoke some manner of pole-vault mumbo jumbo about density and weight and pounds-per-pressure—language which, I determined, the man on the other end of the line understood quite well.

Then there was a call to Tom Jennings, coach of the Pacific Coast

*Track Club for which Billy competes, to check on travel arrange-
ments to the* Los Angeles Times *meet. With the cheers of one triumph hardly quieted, he was looking ahead to the next competition.*

*The schedule Billy Olson was keeping left precious little time for
the savoring of victories.*

*In just a few days he would be off and running again, involved in
one of the most demanding weekends the indoor track-and-field
circuit has to offer. Competing in one meet on Friday and another on
Saturday was commonplace, but the geographic problems posed by
the upcoming schedule needed careful planning.*

*On Friday night he would be in California, involved in what he
himself had judged the most important meet to date. And just as
soon as he finished his vaulting there, he would catch the last flight
from Los Angeles International to New York, where he would compete again the following night.*

*"It's the most difficult double you can do," says Billy's teammate,
Brad Pursley. "If you're going from East to West, from New York to
L.A., it isn't so bad. The time change is in your favor. But if you
compete in Los Angeles first, you lose three hours. It's a killer."*

*The time changes weren't Billy's major concern. Advised that his
flight from Los Angeles to New York was one which required a
layover and plane change in Chicago, he urged Jennings to see if he
couldn't find some airline that had a direct flight. "The landing and
taking off," Billy said, "kills me. With my sinus problem the way it
is right now, the up-and-down stuff makes it feel as if my head's
going to come off. And anytime there's a plane change, the possibility of getting there without my poles increases a good deal."*

Jennings said he would see what he could work out.

*Hanging up the phone, Billy smiled. "All this may be a waste of
time," he said. "It depends on the Russians."*

*Meet officials in Los Angeles and New York were excited about
the arrival of Sergei Bubka and Konstantin Volkov from the Soviet
Union. The anticipated confrontation between Olson and the two
outstanding vaulters from Russia promised great box-office business.*

*For several days, though, Billy had been hearing rumors that
concerned him. Word was that the Soviets would not be at both
meets. One, he had heard, would compete in Los Angeles, while the
other would forego that meet and vault only in New York.*

If that was the case, Olson had already informed meet officials, he would vault only in Los Angeles.

"Over the years," says Don Hood, "Billy's learned to take better care of himself. If a situation like this had come up a couple of years ago, he would have just shrugged and gone ahead with the plan. But now he realizes the importance of not allowing the competition an unfair advantage. He won't duck a head-to-head meeting with anyone, but he has come to realize that it is to his advantage for it to be a fair fight."

"I hope they're both in Los Angeles," Billy said over breakfast. "I'm excited about vaulting against them. If they're both in L.A. we'll go at it, then run for the plane to get to New York. But if one of them is in New York, resting, waiting, I'm going to do my best in Los Angeles and then get on a plane coming back to Texas."

If the upcoming confrontation with the Russian vaulters weighed on Billy's mind, there was little evidence of it as he went about his daily routines. Shortly after noon he drove out to the Abilene Christian campus to work with Coach Hood and the other ACU vaulters in a gymnastics class.

To the untrained eye, it seemed more like a fun-and-games physical education class than serious work as a half-dozen young men went through a series of exercises on the trampoline and rings. There was a lot of good-natured kidding and sharing of news. The college vaulters told Billy of their weekend competition in Albuquerque and asked for details of his Dallas victory.

In one corner of the room, Coach Hood stood watching, his attention seemingly focused on several athletes at once. "I'm just here as a spectator," he says. "These guys don't need me to tell them what to do. They come in here and have a good time, but they get a lot of work done because they're constantly goading each other. Everyone makes everyone else work that much harder. There's a lot of laughing and cutting up, but there's also a lot of competition.

"It is difficult—almost impossible—for a pole vaulter to work alone and expect to improve. He needs other vaulters to measure himself against, others to watch and point out flaws in his form. And then there's the competition that goes on in every phase of a workout. One may be tired and want to cut corners, but he won't

because his buddy is anxious to run one more sprint or vault one more time.

"That, I think, is the main reason Billy's stayed here in Abilene. We've got a number of good vaulters here, and it helps him to be around them. At the same time, it helps to have him around them. It's an ideal situation for all concerned."

Later in the afternoon there was a team meeting where Coach Hood addressed all members of the squad, evaluating performances from the previous weekend's meet and talking at length about goals for the upcoming week.

He had asked Billy to attend and give a report on a young athlete named Brad Urshel, a Princeton graduate and promising decathlon performer who had come to Abilene to train the previous fall.

Urshel had been seriously injured in an automobile accident near San Angelo while en route to a decathlon meet. Rushed to a hospital in Odessa with severe head injuries, he had lain near death. Dallas millionaire H. Ross Perot, a friend of the young man's father, had rushed a team of surgeons from Dallas to attend the youngster. Then, once his condition had stabilized, he had been flown to Dallas in a private medical jet owned by Perot.

While in Dallas for the Times-Herald *meet, Billy had paid Urshel a visit. He told the team gathering of the progress Urshel was making. "His spirits are good and there is every indication that he's eventually going to be okay. But he needs encouragement from us. And he needs our prayers."*

Before the meeting broke up, several members of the ACU squad offered prayers for Brad Urshel's recovery.

It was a moving moment.

Billy, I think, sensed my surprise at the atmosphere inside the cramped dressing room. "Things are different here," he said. "Athletics are important, but not as important as people. That's what makes Coach Hood so good at what he does. In addition to being an outstanding coach, he cares about everyone on his team as an individual. You won't hear him talking down to people. He treats them as equals. I guarantee you he's far more concerned about Brad Urshel's getting well than he is about anyone setting a record or winning a race. That's the kind of man he is."

Then Billy laughed. "He's not at his best today, though. He's going on a couple of hours' sleep. One of the married guys on the team woke him in the middle of the night to ask if he could baby-sit because the guy's wife was having another baby. I don't think he got to bed until about five this morning."

For a community noted for its quiet, slow-moving pace, I thought, the residents of Abilene keep pretty hectic schedules.

And none more hectic than Billy Olson. Following the meeting, there was a workout, then a reporter from Ultra *magazine arrived from the airport to interview him for a piece she was doing on Texas Olympic hopefuls.*

The interview completed, Billy suggested a trip to a favorite bar-becue place for dinner. "Right now," he said, "I'm about five pounds under the weight I need to be, so I'm eating like a horse."

After the meal was completed, he returned to the darkened campus for a weight workout with his fellow vaulters and a handful of ACU football players. It was almost eleven before he returned home.

For a couple of days I shadowed Billy's steps, trying to get some grasp of the demands on his time and energy. For the time being, I determined, Billy Olson was totally dedicated to his sport. Several times he suggested that the 1984 season would be his last, that he looked forward to the time when he could put aside the constantly sore back and other various aches and pains which come with pole vaulting. He talked of settling into a career, possibly in partnership with his father, of playing more golf, of relaxing for the first time in years.

All that, however, would have to wait. His dedication as he awoke each day was evident. If he was to accomplish the final goals he had set for himself, there would be little time for other things.

"Sometimes," says friend Brad Pursley, "I think he almost has tunnel vision about all this. He's more serious than I've ever known him to be. In fact, we've argued about it a few times. But I have tremendous respect for what he's trying to do. And I won't be the least bit surprised to see him accomplish what he's after."

It is that tunnel-vision approach, I have determined, that separates the great athletes from those who only dream of greatness. Dedication is a word bandied about in the sports world in an almost cliché fashion. Coaches preach it endlessly and athletes constantly

speak of the need for it. Few I've known have defined it—and lived
it—as Billy Olson does.

I fought an urge to follow Billy to Los Angeles, to witness firsthand his battle with the young Russian who had taken his indoor
world record from him. But a list of less exciting things demanded
my attention at home.

Thus I bade him farewell and good luck, stopping just short of a
pep talk which he didn't need.

"I've got a good feeling about this weekend," he said.

The Forum, which is located in the Los Angeles suburb of In-
glewood, was abuzz with 11,000 people as the pole-vault competition got underway.

The Soviet delegation, which had arrived in the United States
after a 7,400-mile trip from Moscow, had both Bubka and Volkov
along. Billy was pleased that he would be vaulting against both
Russian vaulters.

Much of the pre-meet publicity had focused on the dual between
Olson and Bubka, the only athletes ever to vault 19 feet indoors.
There were hints of a new record and detailed reports on Bubka's
remarkable accomplishments. He was, insisted a Soviet journalist-
translator who had made the trip, the finest athlete in the world.
"He is Russia's fastest sprinter, with a best of 10.2 in the 100 meters,
and has long jumped over 26 feet," the foreign sportswriter told his
American counterparts.

Certainly he looked the part of a world champion. At 6'2", 186
pounds, he more resembled a wrestler or boxer than a pole vaulter.
And he had a carriage about him that spoke of tremendous confidence in his abilities.

Volkov, who has a working knowledge of the English language,
visited with Olson upon his arrival at the arena and wasted little
time telling him that his fellow countryman had made incredible
strides in the last six months. "At home," he grinned, "we have
begun to call him Superman."

Billy was not smiling.

As he watched Bubka vault he decided the nickname was not
improper. Handling a pole that was considerably longer (17 feet)
than those used by the other competitors, and holding higher (16

feet, 9½ inches), he was clearing the bar with great room to spare on each vault.

"It doesn't seem fair," Billy said to Earl Bell. "This guy's unbelievable. Watching him, you have to believe he's capable of going 20 feet under the right conditions. The minute I saw the pole he was going to use, I knew we were all in big trouble."

When the bar was moved up to 18 feet, 10¾ inches, Bubka cleared it easily, bringing a roar of approval from the stands.

Volkov missed badly on each of his three attempts at the height and was eliminated.

Billy, who had been struggling in the early stages of the competition, having to make seven jumps to keep pace with his Soviet rival, missed on his first attempt at the height. Then, as Bubka waited, Olson missed a second time.

Tom Jennings summoned his vaulter to the stands and made a suggestion. "What you want to do is beat Bubka, not worry about records. Pass on your last try at this height and go after 19-¼. Put some pressure on him."

What he was suggesting was that Olson spend what could amount to his final jump of the competition trying to clear a height he had only managed once before in his life.

There was a hush in the arena as Billy stood at the top of the runway, ready to attempt a height that would equal his American record.

As he slipped over the bar his chest brushed it ever so slightly, but it remained in place. Even before he hit the pit he knew he had made it. The crowd went crazy, marveling at the achievement and aware that finally its favorite in this two-man derby had put the pressure on his adversary.

Bubka silenced the celebration in short order. Continuing the cat-and-mouse game which the competition had become, he informed officials that he would pass at the height Olson had just cleared. He wished the bar raised to 19 feet, 1½ inches. To win, he would have to break his own world record.

Because of the prearranged order of vaulting, Olson was to try the record height first. Raising his grip on his pole three inches, he built up speed down the runway, planted the pole, but lost control half-

*way through the vault. His first attempt had ended before he ever
had a chance to try and get over the bar.*

*Bubka wasted no time getting to the runway for his first attempt.
Waiting for the officials to give him the go-ahead, he bit his bottom
lip and repeatedly adjusted his grip.*

*Then he was off and running, a picture of determined power
rushing toward the moment of truth. Launching himself skyward
amidst the swelling roar of the crowd, he was over the bar with
inches to spare. He, too, gently brushed the bar on his way down but
it remained in place.*

*Olson missed twice more as he attempted clearing the highest
he'd ever vaulted, indoors or out—19 feet, 2½ inches. The competition was over.*

*As Bubka threw kisses to the crowd, Olson marveled at his com-
petitor. "Right now he's just so much better than anyone else. He's
amazing."*

*Tom Jennings, reminding him that he too had put on an im-
pressive show, put his arm around Billy's shoulder. "Hey, pal, you
weren't exactly chopped liver out there yourself."*

*"I've got to go back to the drawing board," Billy replied. "I'm
going home and work on getting stronger. If I'm going to compete
with Bubka, I've got to be able to hold higher on the pole. I'm not
going to beat him holding a foot lower than he does."*

*Having made 12 vaults, Billy was more drained than normal
after a competition. And a hamstring had begun to tighten on his
last vaults. Worried that he might injure himself, he contemplated
bypassing the Saturday night meet in New York.*

*But if he did, there would be hints that he was ducking the pos-
sibility of a second defeat at the hands of Bubka. He decided to take
the seven-hour red-eye flight.*

*With the hamstring bothering him, he failed to clear a height in
New York. Bubka, himself obviously weary from the travel, won the
event with a leap of 18 feet, 8¼ inches, defeating Earl Bell on fewer
misses.*

"He's a remarkable vaulter," Bell said afterward, "but he's not

doing anything Billy and I can't do. There are flaws to his tech-
nique, just as there are in everyone else's.

"I just couldn't believe that he was holding as high on the pole as
everyone was saying, so I took one of mine and laid it down next to
his. He was holding 16 feet and 6 inches, not 16-10. Billy and I can
work up to that before this summer."

On the following Sunday afternoon I received a call from Frank
Estes. Calling from the restaurant he operates in Odessa, he was
upset that the local paper had given only the bare results of the Los
Angeles meet.

"That must have been something to see," he said. "Two guys
going over 19. Man, I wish I'd been there."

I told him what I had learned from several eyewitnesses, describ-
ing Billy's dramatic decision to risk his third jump at 19-¼, then
Bubka's comeback as he vaulted even higher.

Frank was clearly excited. "Just hearing about it makes the hair
stand up on the back of my neck. Those guys are unbelievable. No
telling how high they're going to raise the record before they get
through slugging it out."

We talked for a few minutes more before he grew silent for a time.
"You know," he finally said, "it has to be tough to go 19 feet and lose.
But that's the kind of thing Billy thrives on. He'll go back to work
even harder—be even more determined now. I've seen him do it
before.

"If I were a betting man, I'd give you odds he'll be holding higher
on the pole by spring. He'll be a little stronger and a little faster. I've
never known anyone who responds to a challenge better than Billy.
This Bubka guy had better be ready by the time the Olympics roll
around."

From what I have learned of Billy Olson in recent months, I have
no argument with Frank's observation.

Appendix

BILLY OLSON'S VAULTING PROGRESS

Year	Affiliation	Class	Mark
1973	Lincoln Jr. High	9th grade	10'6"
1975	Abilene High	Junior	14'9"
1976	Abilene High	Senior	15'10"
1977	Unattached	—	17'10¾"
1978	Abilene Christian	Freshman	17'½"
1979	Abilene Christian	Sophomore	18'½"
1980	Abilene Christian	Junior	18'7½"
1981	Pacific Coast Club	—	18'4½"
1982	Abilene Christian	Senior	18'10"
1983	Pacific Coast Club	—	19'¼"
1984	Pacific Coast Club	—	19'¼"